WORLD HISTORY AND GEOGRAPHY
EARLY AGES

CHAPTER TESTS
& LESSON QUIZZES

Mc Graw Hill Education

networks

mheducation.com/prek-12

Send all inquiries to:
McGraw-Hill Education
8787 Orion Place
Columbus, OH 43240

ISBN: 978-0-07-897489-2
MHID: 0-07-897489-5

Printed in the United States of America.

1 2 3 4 5 6 QVS 21 20 19 18 17

Table of Contents

NAME ______________________ DATE ______________ CLASS ____________

Lesson Quiz 1-1

networks

The Rise of Civilization

DIRECTIONS: Modified True/False In the blank, indicate whether the statement is true (T) or false (F). If false, edit the statement to make it a true statement.

______ **1.** An archaeologist might analyze animal remains on stone weapons to learn about prehistoric hunting.

______ **2.** C-14 dating helps reveal the age of an object because living things slowly gain radioactive carbon over time.

______ **3.** Both Paleolithic men and women had to find and acquire food; therefore, it is likely that there was equality between them.

______ **4.** Paleolithic peoples probably lived in small, nuclear family units.

______ **5.** *Homo habilis* is called "handy human" because this early human may have used stone tools.

DIRECTIONS: Multiple Choice Indicate the answer choice that best completes the statement or answers the question.

______ **6.** The best way to describe Paleolithic peoples and their way of life is by calling them

A. artifacts.
B. hominids.
C. nomads.
D. prehistoric.

______ **7.** Which of the following is a study of past societies through an analysis of what people have left behind?

A. history
B. radiocarbon dating
C. fossil analysis
D. archaeology

NAME______________________ DATE ______________ CLASS __________

Lesson Quiz 1-2

networks

The Rise of Civilization

DIRECTIONS: Completion Enter the appropriate word(s) to complete the statement.

1. The Neolithic Revolution was the shift from hunting and gathering to ____________________ in various parts of the world.

2. A reliable source of meat, milk, and wool resulted from the ____________________ of animals.

3. When humans first settled in farming villages, their ____________________ became more complex.

4. The first civilizations developed in ____________________.

5. ____________________ brought new civilizations in contact with one another.

DIRECTIONS: Multiple Choice Indicate the answer choice that best completes the statement or answers the question.

________ **6.** The change that led to all other changes in the Neolithic Revolution was the

A. movement away from eating only fruits and grains to eating meat.
B. discovery of new technology.
C. change in the method of obtaining food.
D. development of social structures.

________ **7.** The use of metal tools marked the end of the Neolithic Age and a

A. beginning of the Metal Age.
B. movement away from agriculture.
C. complete abandonment of other tools.
D. new level of human control over the environment and its resources.

________ **8.** The Neolithic Revolution was followed by the

A. Ice Age.
B. Paleolithic Age.
C. Mesolithic Age.
D. Bronze Age.

________ **9.** Which of the following is the most complete definition of a civilization?

A. any culture that uses written records and whose people practice a religion
B. the gathering of human groups in farms, villages, and settlements
C. any social structure based on economic power
D. a complex culture in which a large number of humans share elements in common

Lesson Quiz 1-3

networks

The Rise of Civilization

DIRECTIONS: Matching Match each item with the correct statement below.

_______ **1.** a government by divine authority

_______ **2.** a religious and political power center of the city-state

_______ **3.** a Sumerian innovation used for recordkeeping

_______ **4.** a Sumerian innovation used to create finely crafted metalwork

_______ **5.** rich soil deposited by rivers during a flood

A. bronze
B. cuneiform
C. theocracy
D. silt
E. ziggurat

DIRECTIONS: Multiple Choice Indicate the answer choice that best completes the statement or answers the question.

_______ **6.** Which statement is most accurate?

A. The flooding of the Tigris and Euphrates was the main factor that led to civilization in Mesopotamia.
B. The melting of snows in the upland mountains was the main factor that led to civilization in Mesopotamia.
C. Irrigation and drainage ditches were the main factors that led to civilization in Mesopotamia.
D. The flooding of the Tigris and Euphrates and the ability to control flooding were the main factors that led to civilization in Mesopotamia.

_______ **7.** The most important physical structure in a Sumerian city-state was the

A. city hall.
B. temple.
C. cuneiform.
D. irrigation ditch.

_______ **8.** Which of the following was an impact of geography on Mesopotamian culture?

A. theocratic government
B. the city-state political structure
C. cities that were defended
D. buildings made of mud bricks

_______ **9.** The greatest new development made by Sumerians was

A. cuneiform.
B. silt.
C. civilization.
D. bronze.

NAME ________________________ DATE ______________ CLASS __________

Chapter 1 Test, Form A

networks

The Rise of Civilization

DIRECTIONS: Matching Match each item with the correct statement below.

_______ **1.** the arc of rich soil between the Mediterranean Sea and the Persian Gulf

_______ **2.** a Neolithic farming village

_______ **3.** a massive stepped tower

_______ **4.** a king or queen

_______ **5.** period before writing was developed

_______ **6.** Sumerian writing system

_______ **7.** large city-state in Mesopotamia

_______ **8.** a skilled worker

_______ **9.** an object made by humans that sheds light on the past

_______ **10.** site of the discovery of a 1.8-million-year-old hominid

A. cuneiform

B. Fertile Crescent

C. Olduvai Gorge

D. Çatalhüyük

E. prehistory

F. artifact

G. Uruk

H. ziggurat

I. artisan

J. monarch

DIRECTIONS: Multiple Choice Indicate the answer choice that best completes the statement or answers the question.

_______ **11.** Where do scientists believe that *Homo sapiens sapiens* first appeared between 150,000 and 200,000 years ago?

A. North America

B. Africa

C. Asia

D. Europe

_______ **12.** The inhabitants of what are now Mexico and Central America were

A. priests.

B. Neanderthals.

C. Sumerians.

D. Mesoamericans.

Chapter 1 Test, Form A *cont.*

networks

The Rise of Civilization

_______ **13.** Because trade brought new civilizations into contact with one another,

A. early river valley civilizations developed independently.

B. painting and sculpture were developed.

C. the transfer of new technology often occurred.

D. rulers claimed that their power was based on divine approval.

_______ **14.** Who were the first hominids to learn to make fires deliberately?

A. *Homo habilis*

B. *Homo sapiens*

C. *Homo sapiens sapiens*

D. *Australopithecus*

_______ **15.** The ability to acquire food on a regular basis meant that humans

A. had less control over their environment.

B. could give up nomadic ways of life and begin to live in settled communities.

C. could use animals as pets.

D. could use fire to cook their food.

_______ **16.** Anthropology is the study of

A. underground insects.

B. tools and weapons.

C. human life and culture.

D. ancient texts.

_______ **17.** A main characteristic of civilizations is

A. art.

B. the family.

C. use of fire.

D. use of tools.

_______ **18.** Which of the following did the Sumerians invent?

A. calculus

B. irrigation

C. the sundial

D. the umbrella

_______ **19.** What were the basic political units of Sumerian civilization?

A. ziggurats

B. monarchs

C. cuneiform

D. city-states

_______ **20.** How did people in the Fertile Crescent adapt to their environment?

A. by hunting and gathering

B. by sifting through the silt

C. by using irrigation and drainage

D. by abandoning the river valleys when necessary

DIRECTIONS: Short Answer Answer each of the following questions.

21. Explain in detail how anthropologists and archaeologists might find, examine, and date a hominid discovery today.

____

____

____

> In Uruk [Gilgamesh] built walls.... the outer wall where the cornice runs, it shines with the brilliance of copper; and the inner wall, it has no equal! Climb upon the wall of Uruk; walk along it, I say; regard the foundation terrace and examine the masonry: is it not burned brick and good. The seven sages laid the foundations.
>
> —*The Epic of Gilgamesh*

22. Of what aspect or aspects of civilization is the speaker most proud in this quotation? What does the quotation suggest about the place within the walls?

____

____

____

NAME_________________________ DATE ______________ CLASS ___________

Chapter 1 Test, Form B

networks

The Rise of Civilization

DIRECTIONS: Short Answer Answer each of the following questions on a separate piece of paper.

The Spread of Systematic Agriculture

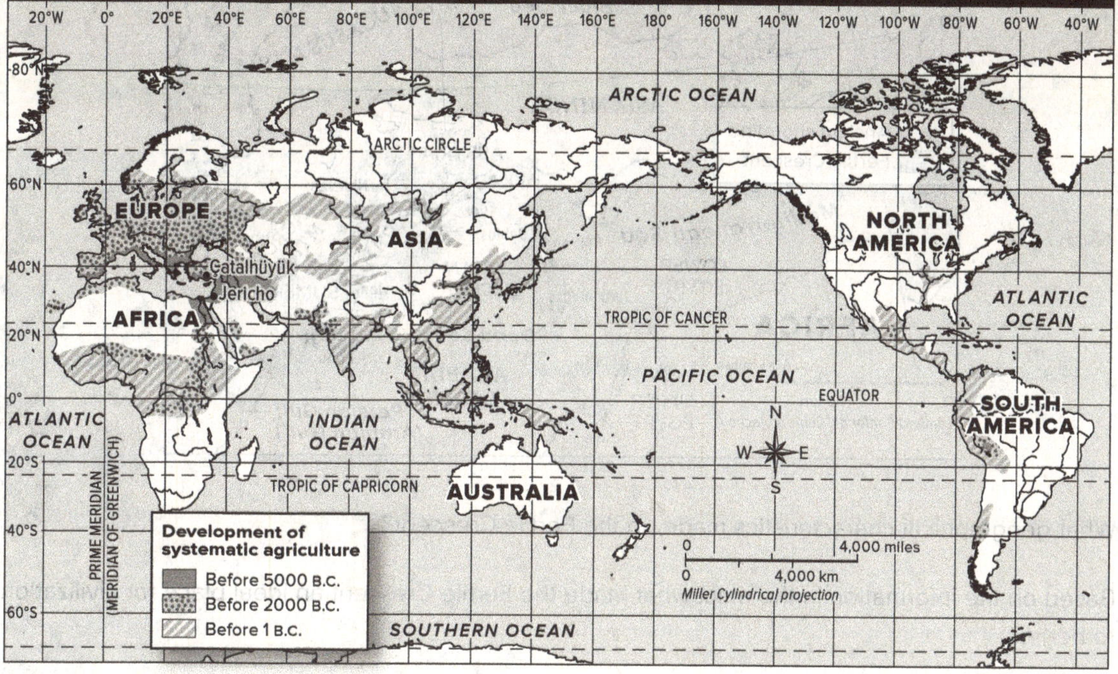

1. Using the map, identify the place where systematic agriculture arose, and name three places where it spread before 2000 B.C.

2. What geographical factors account for the spread of agriculture before 2000 B.C.?

Early Human Civilizations' Tools and Their Effects	
Tool	**Effect**
spear, bow and arrow	made hunting easier
bone harpoon and fishhook	increased the catch of fish
bone needles	made it possible to make nets and baskets and to sew hides together for clothing
sharp-edge tools	made it easier to cut and dig
scraping tools	made it easier to clean animal hides

3. Using the information from the chart, what conclusion can you draw about why early peoples created the tools listed?

4. Which tools were probably used for hunting and fishing? Which tools were used for gathering?

NAME ______________________ DATE ______________ CLASS __________

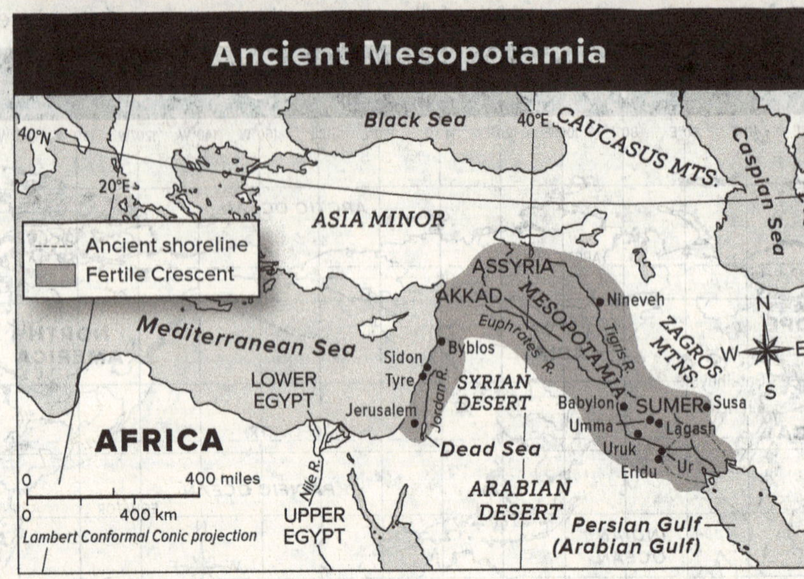

5. What geographical characteristics made up the Fertile Crescent?

6. Based on the information in the map, what made the Fertile Crescent an ideal place for civilization to begin?

DIRECTIONS: Essay Answer the following question on a separate piece of paper.

7. A civilization is defined as a complex culture in which large numbers of people share a number of common elements such as social structure, religion and art. The development of systematic agriculture allowed people to settle together and develop as a civilization. Using information presented in this chapter, explain this statement: Early humans were nomadic hunter-gatherers, but as they developed agricultural skills, they settled and formed the first civilizations along fertile river valleys.

NAME________________________________ DATE ________________ CLASS ____________

Lesson Quiz 2-1

networks

The Spread of Civilization

DIRECTIONS: Matching Match each item with the correct statement below.

________ **1.** complex system of writing, meaning "sacred writings," that is made up of pictures and more abstract forms

________ **2.** part of a large complex of buildings dedicated to the dead

________ **3.** way in which dead bodies of wealthy Egyptians were preserved from the time of the Old Kingdom

________ **4.** title of Egyptian monarch who possessed absolute power

________ **5.** administrative organization with officials and regular procedures that helped run the government

A. pharaoh

B. hieroglyphics

C. mummification

D. bureaucracy

E. pyramids

DIRECTIONS: Multiple Choice Indicate the answer choice that best completes the statement or answers the question.

________ **6.** Egyptian history is divided into three major periods, known as the

A. Upper, Lower, and Middle Kingdoms.
B. Old, Middle, and New Kingdoms.
C. Early, Middle, and Last Kingdoms.
D. Old, Middle, and Oldest Kingdoms.

________ **7.** The development of Egyptian civilization was influenced most powerfully by

A. the Nile River.
B. the building of pyramids.
C. monogamous marriage laws.
D. invasions from other peoples.

________ **8.** The Egyptians developed an accurate 365-day calendar by basing their year on

A. the pharaoh's worship of the sun god.
B. old Sumerian calculations of weather.
C. information found in Egyptian pyramids.
D. the movements of the moon and the star Sirius.

________ **9.** Religion provided the Egyptians with a sense of security, and Egyptian rulers were viewed as

A. manifestations of the land god.
B. earthly forms of the sun god Re.
C. disruptions in the universal cosmic order.
D. the sole gods to be worshipped in Egyptian society.

NAME________________________ DATE______________ CLASS__________

Lesson Quiz 2-2

networks

The Spread of Civilization

DIRECTIONS: Matching Match each item with the correct statement below.

________ **1.** migrating groups who domesticated animals for food, shelter, and clothing and who also helped spread language, goods, and technology

________ **2.** religious teachers whose words became a source of ideals for social justice as they condemned the rich for causing the poor to suffer

________ **3.** traders who lived in a narrow strip of land along the eastern Mediterranean coast and devised an alphabet with 22 different characters representing sounds

________ **4.** a distinct group organized in tribes that established the religion of Judaism, which later influenced both Christianity and Islam

________ **5.** a rich civilization that built an enormous palace at Knossos on the island of

A. Phoenicians

B. prophets

C. Minoans

D. pastoral nomads

E. Israelites

DIRECTIONS: Multiple Choice Indicate the answer choice that best completes the statement or answers the question.

________ **6.** The Minoans established

A. a temple in Jerusalem.

B. a far-ranging sea-empire based on trade.

C. an alphabet that was passed on to the Greeks.

D. the Hittite kingdom, with its capital at Hattushash.

________ **7.** Significant nomadic peoples who spoke a language derived from a single parent tongue were the

A. Israelites. **C.** Indo-Europeans.

B. Minoans. **D.** Phoenicians.

________ **8.** The Hittites were the first Indo-Europeans to

A. use iron weapons.

B. create a trading empire.

C. build a labyrinth similar to that of King Minos.

D. believe in one God who created the world and everything in it.

________ **9.** The Phoenicians produced a number of goods for foreign markets, including purple dye, glass, and

A. pottery. **C.** silver jewelry.

B. lumber. **D.** ivory figurines.

NAME________________________________ DATE _______________ CLASS __________

Lesson Quiz 2-3

networks

The Spread of Civilization

DIRECTIONS: Matching Match each item with the correct statement below.

_________ **1.** Indo-European written language that developed in the Indus Valley around 1000 B.C.

_________ **2.** descendants of the Indus Valley people

_________ **3.** carefully planned ancient cities of the Indus River valley that flourished for hundreds of years

_________ **4.** Indo-speaking nomadic peoples with a strong warrior tradition who at first settled in northern India but later controlled all of India

_________ **5.** the highest mountains in the world, found in the far north of India

A. Himalaya

B. Aryans

C. Sanskrit

D. Harrapa and Mohenjo-daro

E. Dravidians

DIRECTIONS: Multiple Choice Indicate the answer choice that best completes the statement or answers the question.

_________ **6.** Rich soil to grow wheat, parley, and peas in the Indus Valley resulted from

A. the annual flooding of the Indus River.

B. proximity to the Arabian Sea.

C. a sophisticated irrigation system.

D. importing soil from the Deccan Plateau.

_________ **7.** Early Indian writings that reveal that India was a world of many small kingdoms between 1500 B.C. and 400 B.C. are called the

A. citadel.

B. monsoon.

C. suttee.

D. Vedas.

_________ **8.** Public wells for supplying water to city residents, an advanced drainage system, and a system of garbage disposal in Indus Valley cities are indications of

A. intense competition among tribes.

B. an organized government.

C. a strong warrior tradition.

D. a change from a nomadic lifestyle to farming.

_________ **9.** Harrappan rulers based their power on

A. a strong military.

B. a generous distribution of wealth.

C. a belief in divine assistance.

D. a democratic system of government.

NAME_________________________________ DATE _________________ CLASS __________

Lesson Quiz 2-4

networks

The Spread of Civilization

DIRECTIONS: Matching Match each item with the correct statement below.

_________ **1.** characters in Chinese in which picture or character symbols are combined to represent ideas—for example, showing the sun rising behind the trees to represent "east"

_________ **2.** the second Chinese dynasty, which was mostly a farming society but was also concerned with warfare

_________ **3.** the duty of members of a family to subordinate their needs and desires to those of the male head of the family

_________ **4.** characters or picture symbols in the Chinese language that represent an object, like a mountain of the Sun

_________ **5.** the longest-lasting Chinese dynasty, which ruled for almost 800 years and claimed it possessed the Mandate of Heaven to rule

A. pictographs

B. filial piety

C. Shang

D. ideographs

E. Zhou

DIRECTIONS: Multiple Choice Indicate the answer choice that best completes the statement or answers the question.

_________ **6.** On their northern and western frontiers, the Chinese people were isolated from people in other parts of Asia by

A. lakes and rivers.

B. the South China Sea.

C. mountains and deserts.

D. the Bay of Bengal.

_________ **7.** In the northern frontier regions of ancient China, conflicts arose between the Chinese and the

A. Indians. **C.** Japanese.

B. Mongolians. **D.** Koreans.

_________ **8.** During the Shang dynasty, the class of people that owned the land and waged war were the

A. peasants. **C.** merchants.

B. slaves. **D.** aristocrats.

_________ **9.** The basic economic and social unit in ancient China was the

A. family. **C.** artisans.

B. dynasty. **D.** bureaucracy.

NAME_________________________________ DATE _______________ CLASS ___________

Lesson Quiz 2-5

networks

The Spread of Civilization

DIRECTIONS: Matching Match each item with the correct statement below.

_______ **1.** a South American civilization that built an impressive solar observatory made up of thirteen stone towers on a hillside north of Lima, Peru

_______ **2.** the oldest major city in the Americas which appeared around 2500 B.C.

_______ **3.** a Mesoamerican civilization whose center at Monte Albán contained temples and pyramids atop a 1,200-foot-high mountain

_______ **4.** first major city in Mesoamerica, located about 30 miles northeast of present-day Mexico City

_______ **5.** the oldest known Mesoamerican civilization, which appeared around 1200 B.C.

A. Zapotec

B. Teotihuacán

C. Caral

D. Olmec

E. Chavin

DIRECTIONS: Multiple Choice Indicate the answer choice that best completes the statement or answers the question.

_______ **6.** Another name for the "rubber people" who grew rubber trees along the coast of the Gulf of Mexico south of Veracruz was the

A. Olmec.
B. Zapotec.
C. Chavin.
D. Inca.

_______ **7.** In which ancient Mesoamerican civilization did about 20,000 people live in terraces cut into the sides of a mountain?

A. Olmec
B. Zapotec
C. Chavin
D. Maya

_______ **8.** The Maya adapted a ceremonial ball game played on a stone court, worship of a jaguar-like god, a calendar, and a numeric system from the

A. Inca.
B. Chavin.
C. Olmec.
D. Zapotec.

_______ **9.** Teotihuacán was a busy trade center known for objects made of

A. iron.
B. bronze.
C. obsidian.
D. silver.

NAME________________________________ DATE __________________ CLASS ____________

Chapter 2 Test, Form A

networks

The Spread of Civilization

DIRECTIONS: Matching Match each item with the correct statement below.

_______ **1.** the key to China's social system

_______ **2.** the period during which the Great Pyramid of King Khufu at Giza was constructed, showing the power of the Egyptian pharaohs

_______ **3.** the upper class in Shang society whose wealth was land-based and who passed power from one generation to the next

_______ **4.** the geographic feature that isolated China from India

_______ **5.** the group that gave up their nomadic lifestyle for farming in the process of settling in India

_______ **6.** the cradle of Indian civilization, which enjoyed a moderate climate in ancient times

_______ **7.** the center of the Zapotec civilization

_______ **8.** the longest river in the world, the annual flooding of which left a rich deposit of mud that enriched the soil and allowed Egyptian farmers to grow a surplus of food

_______ **9.** an important river in India, with a valley that was cultivated for its rich farmland after the invention of the iron plow made it possible to clear the dense growth along its banks

_______ **10.** a Mesoamerican civilization that pre-dated the Maya

A. Himalaya

B. Nile

C. Aryans

D. Monte Albán

E. Ganges

F. male supremacy

G. Old Kingdom

H. Olmec

I. aristocracy

J. Indus Valley

DIRECTIONS: Multiple Choice Indicate the answer choice that best completes the statement or answers the question.

_______ **11.** Egyptian society, with the god-king at the top, was organized like

A. a pyramid.

B. the Nile River.

C. hieroglyphic script.

D. Upper and Lower Egypt.

_______ **12.** Hieratic script, a simplified version of Egyptian hieroglyphic writing, was used

A. by peasants who were too uneducated to read hieroglyphs.

B. only by the nobles, as a way of communicating with the gods.

C. by the blind, as a type of Braille.

D. for business transactions, record keeping, and the general needs of daily life.

_______ **13.** The "ten lost tribes" were

A. scattered Israelite tribes.

B. the Sea Peoples.

C. ten ancient cities.

D. Egyptian traders.

_______ **14.** Unlike other religions of the time, political leaders in Israel

A. were believed to be directly descended from God, and therefore almost gods.

B. were required to burn the sacred texts after they read them.

C. were the sole authority on religious matters.

D. could not claim they alone knew the will of God, because the Jewish teachings were written down for anyone to read.

_______ **15.** A civilization in the Eastern Mediterranean that built structures similar to the labyrinth of King Minos was the

A. Israelite civilization.

B. Egyptian civilization.

C. Minoan civilization.

D. Phoenician civilization.

_______ **16.** Religion and political power were closely linked in early Indian civilization, as is indicated by the combination of the royal palace and the holy temple in the citadel, or fortress, at

A. Harappa.

B. Calcutta.

C. Mohenjo-daro.

D. the Deccan Plateau.

_______ **17.** It was believed that the king was the link between Heaven and Earth during the

A. Xia dynasty.

B. Shang dynasty.

C. Zhou dynasty.

D. Qin dynasty.

_______ **18.** The Chinese had developed a simple script with a form that was mainly pictographic and ideographic by the time of the

A. Xia dynasty.

B. Shang dynasty.

C. Zhou dynasty.

D. Qin dynasty.

_______ **19.** A city that appeared around 2500 B.C. in the Supe River valley of Peru, in which stone buildings were used for official business, as apartment buildings, and as grand residences, was

A. Caral.

B. Harappa.

C. Teotihuacán.

D. Monte Albán.

_______ **20.** Most of the people in the Mesoamerican city of Teotihuacán were

A. skilled artisans.

B. priests.

C. farmers.

D. members of the ruling class.

_______ **21.** A basic principle of Chinese government, which allows a revolution to overthrow and replace a corrupt ruler, is called

A. filial piety.

B. ancestor worship.

C. the Mandate of Heaven.

D. the ideograph.

_______ **22.** Around 900 B.C., the Chavin people built a temple surrounded by two pyramids and stone figures depicting different gods in the coastal regions of what is now

A. Brazil.

B. Mexico.

C. Central America.

D. Peru and Ecuador.

Chapter 2 Test, Form A *cont.*

The Spread of Civilization

DIRECTIONS: Short Answer Answer each of the following questions.

> At one time scholars believed that the civilization of ancient Egypt was the first in the history of the world and the progenitor of all others. We now know this to be untrue, but the ancient Egyptians retain one unique distinction: they were the first people on earth to create a nationstate....This state served as the framework of a culture of extraordinary strength, assurance, and durability which lasted for 3,000 years and retained almost to the end of its own unmistakable purity of style.
>
> —Paul Johnson, from *The Civilization of Ancient Egypt,* 1999

23. From the quotation above, what can you infer about the structure of Egyptian society?

______

______

______

> One of the greatest, if not the greatest glory of the Phoenicians was the spread of the alphabet in the Mediterranean area. There is no doubt that the Phoenicians taught the alphabet to the Greeks, nor that the Phoenicians and Greeks were responsible for spreading it in the West....This is certain, and gives the Phoenicians an important role in the history of civilization.
>
> —Sabatino Moscati, from *The World of the Phoenicians,* 1965

24. According to the quotation above, what was the single most important contribution of the Phoenicians? How did the Phoenicians affect other civilizations? What might have happened had the Phoenicians not made this important contribution to civilization?

______

______

______

NAME ______________________ DATE ______________ CLASS ____________

Chapter 2 Test, Form B

networks

The Spread of Civilization

DIRECTIONS: Short Answer Answer each of the following questions on a separate piece of paper.

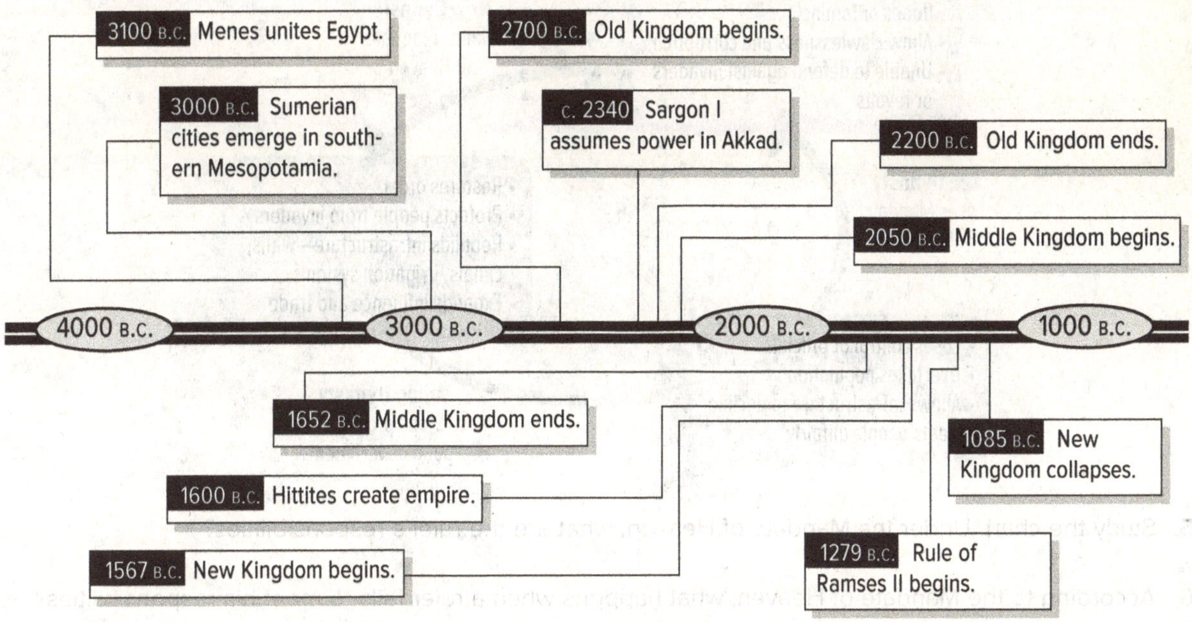

1. Study the time line. How many years did the Old Kingdom last? How many years elapsed between the end of the Old Kingdom and the beginning of the Middle Kingdom?

2. According to the timeline, name one Egyptian ruler who governed during the New Kingdom?

> O whatever god ordained this flight
> Do thou show mercy and return me to the Residence!
> Perhaps thou wilt let me see the place in which my heart dwells!
> What is more important than that I should be buried in Egypt, since I was born there?
> This is an appeal for help. May good fortune befall,
> May God grant me peace, may he do thus to perfect the end of him whom he has afflicted, taking pity on him who he cast out to live Abroad!
> Is he now appeased?
> May he hear the prayer of one far away!
> May he turn his hand from him whom he sent roaming the earth,
> Back to the place when he drew it forth!
>
> —Miriam Lichthiem, trans. *The Story of Sinuhe,* from *Land of Enchanters,* 2001

3. Who does Sinuhe say is responsible for his flight from his homeland in Egypt? Which words from the passage support your answer?

4. What do Sinuhe's words reveal about the role of religion in Egyptian life?

Chapter 2 Test, Form B *cont.*

networks

The Spread of Civilization

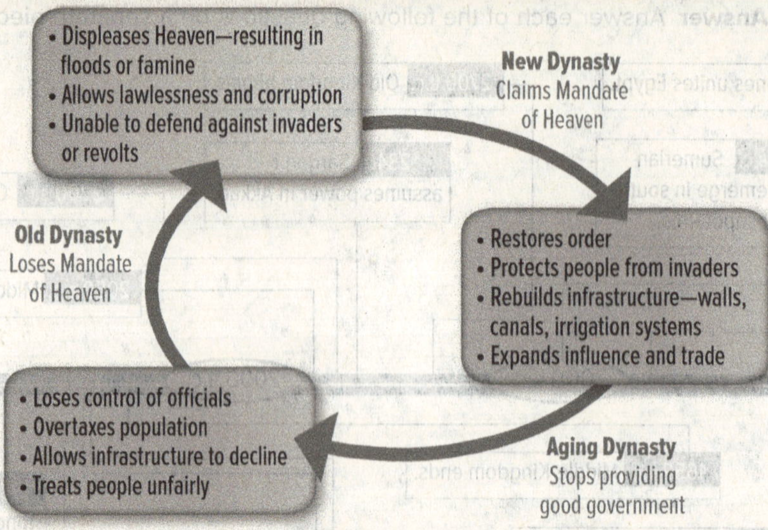

5. Study the chart. Under the Mandate of Heaven, what are the ruler's responsibilities?

6. According to the Mandate of Heaven, what happens when a ruler fails to meet his responsibilities?

DIRECTIONS: Essay Answer the following question on a separate piece of paper.

7. Consider how new techniques in agriculture as well as the use of tools and weaponry have helped early civilizations in Asia and the Americas develop their own unique cultures. Use these details to analyze the chapter's Enduring Understanding statement: *As new techniques in agriculture, toolmaking, and weaponry spread, early civilizations in Asia and the Americas developed unique cultures with complex political, artistic, and philosophical traditions.*

Lesson Quiz 3-1

networks

Early Empires in the Ancient Near East

DIRECTIONS: Modified True/False In the blank, indicate whether the statement is true (T) or false (F). If false edit the statement to make it a true statement.

_______ **1.** In establishing his empire, Sargon executed the ruler of every Sumerian city-state he conquered.

____

____

_______ **2.** Hammurabi established his imperial capital in Babylon.

____

____

_______ **3.** Hammurabi's Code protected people against false accusations. If someone brought a charge but then failed to prove it, the accuser would be punished.

____

____

_______ **4.** After the fall of the Akkadian empire, only a few decades passed before the Babylonian empire arose.

____

____

_______ **5.** The Code of Hammurabi reveals that in ancient Babylon a marriage was decided upon by the two young people who wanted to wed.

____

____

DIRECTIONS: Multiple Choice Indicate the answer choice that best completes the statement or answers the question.

_______ **6.** The term for a large political unit or state, usually under a single leader, controlling many peoples or territories is

A. a city-state.
B. an empire.
C. the Code of Hammurabi.
D. a satrapy.

_______ **7.** Around 2340 B.C., the Sumerian city-states were conquered by the Akkadians under their leader

A. Sargon.
B. Hammurabi.
C. Darius.
D. Zoroaster.

NAME _______________ DATE _______________ CLASS _______________

Lesson Quiz 3-2

networks

Early Empires in the Ancient Near East

DIRECTIONS: Completion Enter the appropriate word(s) to complete the statement.

1. The boy pharaoh who restored worship of the old gods in the New Kingdom was named _______________.

2. _______________ tried to force the Egyptians to worship a single god, Aten.

3. The pharaoh Ahmose I was able to drive the _______________ out of Egypt around 1550 B.C. and establish the New Kingdom.

4. When the _______________ were driven out of Egypt, they returned to their original lands to the south and built a successful trading empire.

5. After the Egyptian Empire fell, it became a part of the empire of _______________.

DIRECTIONS: Multiple Choice Indicate the answer choice that best completes the statement or answers the question.

_____ **6.** Having been conquered by the Hyksos was not all bad for the Egyptians because the Hyksos taught the Egyptians

A. how to make bronze weapons and showed them the advantages of horse-drawn war chariots.

B. how to farm the fertile land in the area.

C. how to build roads to connect the parts of the kingdom.

D. how to cut large blocks of stone, a skill they would use to build the pyramids.

_____ **7.** During the New Kingdom, the Egyptian Empire reached its peak. What was one way it showed its power?

A. The pharaohs sent messengers out to proclaim their achievements throughout the empire.

B. Egyptian armies made a point of looting and destroying their enemies' homes and villages.

C. The pharaohs built a vast library to celebrate their wisdom and intellectual achievements.

D. The pharaohs constructed huge, magnificent temples and statues in their own honor.

_____ **8.** Although the pharaoh Ramses II tried to maintain the Egyptian Empire's strength, he failed because he was unable to hold out against

A. the Hyksos.

B. the Sea Peoples.

C. the Akkadians.

D. the Assyrians.

NAME________________________ DATE ______________ CLASS ___________

Lesson Quiz 3-3

networks

Early Empires in the Ancient Near East

DIRECTIONS: Matching Match each item with the correct statement below.

_______ **1.** site of one of the world's first libraries

_______ **2.** Persian route from Lydia to Susa

_______ **3.** site of the Hanging Gardens

_______ **4.** Persian religion

_______ **5.** king who extended the Persian Empire to India

A. Royal Road

B. Nineveh

C. Babylon

D. Darius

E. Zoroastrianism

DIRECTIONS: Multiple Choice Indicate the answer choice that best completes the statement or answers the question.

_______ **6.** The king of the Chaldeans who rebuilt Babylon was

A. Cyrus.

B. Nebuchadnezzar II.

C. Darius.

D. Ahuramazda.

_______ **7.** The prophet Zoroaster taught that

A. the sun god Aten was the supreme god.

B. the spirits Ahuramazda and Ahriman were allies.

C. all people would attain paradise at the Last Judgment.

D. humans had free choice.

_______ **8.** Cyrus was called "the Great" because he

A. showed no mercy to enemies.

B. had no respect for other cultures.

C. was a large man.

D. showed wisdom and compassion.

_______ **9.** One example of the Assyrians' efficiency and effectiveness as administrators was

A. their system of carrying messages quickly, which involved a network of staging posts and relays of horses.

B. the speed with which they decided whether to execute prisoners of war.

C. their tendency to destroy features such as dams and cut down their enemies' fruit trees.

D. their willingness to allow different cultures to coexist peacefully in their empire.

NAME ________________________ DATE ________________ CLASS ____________

Chapter 3 Test, Form A

networks

Early Empires in the Ancient Near East

DIRECTIONS: Matching Match each item with the correct statement below.

_______ **1.** the Chaldean king who restored Babylon to glory

_______ **2.** the name of Kush while it was still a part of the Egyptian Empire

_______ **3.** the leader who established the world's first empire

_______ **4.** a large political unit, usually with a single leader, that controls many territories

_______ **5.** the pharaoh who later changed his name to Akhenaten

_______ **6.** the ruler of a province in the Persian empire

_______ **7.** the empire ruled by Cyrus the Great

_______ **8.** invaders who attacked the Egyptian Empire during its final days of power

_______ **9.** a people known for using terror as an instrument of warfare

_______ **10.** a city in Kush

A. Nubia

B. Persia

C. Assyrians

D. Meroë

E. Sargon

F. Amenhotep IV

G. Sea Peoples

H. Nebuchadnezzar II

I. satrap

J. empire

DIRECTIONS: Multiple Choice Indicate the answer choice that best completes the statement or answers the question.

_______ **11.** The first empire in world history was

A. the Sumerian empire.
B. the Babylonian empire.
C. the Akkadian empire.
D. the Egyptian empire.

_______ **12.** Hammurabi is remembered for

A. cutting off his son's hand because his son hit him.
B. establishing a collection of laws for Mesopotamian society.
C. teaching the Mesopotamians to forge iron.
D. overthrowing the Akkadian empire.

_______ **13.** Cyrus the Great showed such wisdom and compassion when he conquered Babylon that

A. even the rulers of unconquered states offered to join his empire.

B. everyone accepted him as ruler.

C. he was worshipped as a god.

D. his subjects ridiculed him as too weak to rule.

_______ **14.** Which leader of the Persian empire expanded it into the largest empire the world had yet seen?

A. Cambyses

B. Cyrus

C. Darius

D. Nebuchadnezzar II

_______ **15.** Which of the following contributed to the efficient system of communication that was crucial to sustaining the Persian Empire?

A. well-maintained roads and way stations to provide food, shelter, and fresh horses for traveling officials.

B. trained dogs that carried messages to and from the king over distances as great as 500 miles.

C. the elite foot soldiers and cavalry known as the Immortals.

D. the imposition of a single language throughout the empire.

_______ **16.** The empire that Sargon established was continued by his grandson _____ but fell less than 100 years after his grandson's death.

A. Ramses II.

B. Hammurabi.

C. Cambyses.

D. Naram-Sin.

_______ **17.** In Hammurabi's code, punishments generally followed the principle of retaliation, or the idea that one must

A. give an eye for an eye and a tooth for a tooth.

B. add insult to injury.

C. pay money to atone for wrongdoing.

D. give one's firstborn son to one's victim.

_______ **18.** While the Hyksos attacked the Egyptians from horse-drawn chariots, the Egyptian soldiers were limited to

A. running away.

B. throwing stones.

C. donkey carts.

D. slingshots.

Early Empires in the Ancient Near East

_______ **19.** Why did the Egyptians resist Akhenaten's religious reforms?

A. They wanted to worship a single god, but not Aten.

B. They accepted many gods, and did not like the idea of rejecting or destroying them to worship only one god.

C. They wanted Akhenaten to pay them to convert to his religion.

D. They thought Aten was a false god.

_______ **20.** The Assyrians had the first large armies who carried weapons made of

A. wood.

B. stone.

C. bronze.

D. iron.

_______ **21.** The Code of Hammurabi paints a portrait of a society in which

A. people can do pretty much whatever they want to.

B. almost anything that can go wrong is addressed by one law or another.

C. it is easy to avoid being robbed because one can recognize thieves by their missing hands.

D. the citizens live in fear of being punished.

_______ **22.** What is most unusual about the pharaoh Hatshepsut?

A. Hatshepsut's official statues portray the pharaoh as having a beard.

B. Hatshepsut was interested in mining enterprises.

C. Hatshepsut was a woman.

D. Hatshepsut built an impressive temple near Thebes.

_______ **23.** Darius's elite cavalry and infantry forces were known as the Immortals because

A. they were actually immortal.

B. they were so skilled that it was difficult to kill them in battle.

C. whenever a soldier was killed, he was immediately replaced.

D. they had been guaranteed a place in paradise if they were killed in battle.

DIRECTIONS: Short Answer Answer each of the following questions.

> If anyone commits a robbery and is caught, then he shall be put to death.... If a man put out the eye of another man, his eye shall be put out.
>
> —*The Code of Hammurabi,* c. 1760 B.C.

24. Read the excerpt from the Code of Hammurabi above. Use this information and what you know from the chapter to discuss the importance of the code and how it helps us to understand the social conditions in Mesopotamia.

____

____

____

____

> I had in harness for the forces of my land more chariots and teams of horses than ever before. To Assyria I added land and to its people I added people. I brought contentment to my people [and] provided them with a secure abode.
>
> Tiglath-pileser, exalted prince, the one whom the gods Ashur and Ninurta have continually guided wherever he wished [to go] and who pursued each and every one of the enemies of the god Ashur and laid low all the rebellious.
>
> —Tiglath-pileser I, King of Assyria c. 1100 B.C.

25. The quotation above is attributed to one of the Assyrian emperors. Use this information and what you have read in the chapter to discuss the reputation the Assyrian emperors made for themselves. What did they consider important in the way they built up their empires? What were the strengths and weaknesses of their approach?

____

____

____

____

NAME________________________ DATE______________ CLASS__________

Chapter 3 Test, Form B

networks

Early Empires in the Ancient Near East

DIRECTIONS: Short Answer Answer each of the following questions on a separate piece of paper.

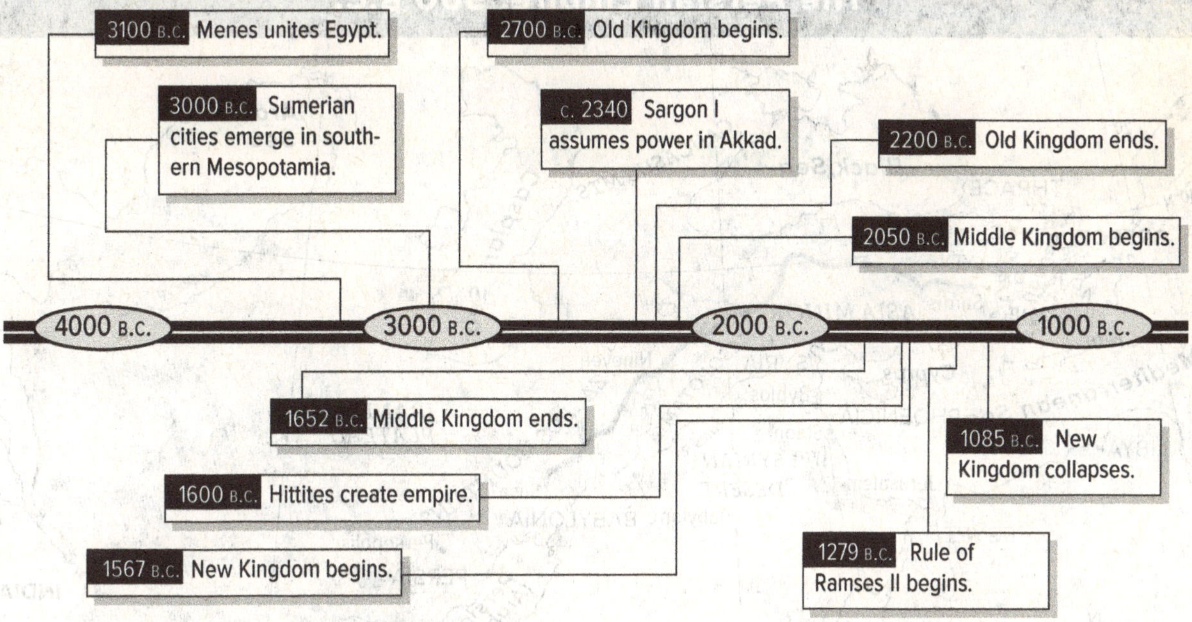

1. Examine the time line above. How many years did the Sumerian city-states exist in Mesopotamia before Sargon's empire building began to threaten their existence?

2. Examine the time line above. How many years did the New Kingdom last in Egypt?

Chapter 3 Test, Form B *cont.*

networks

Early Empires in the Ancient Near East

The Persian Empire, 500 B.C.

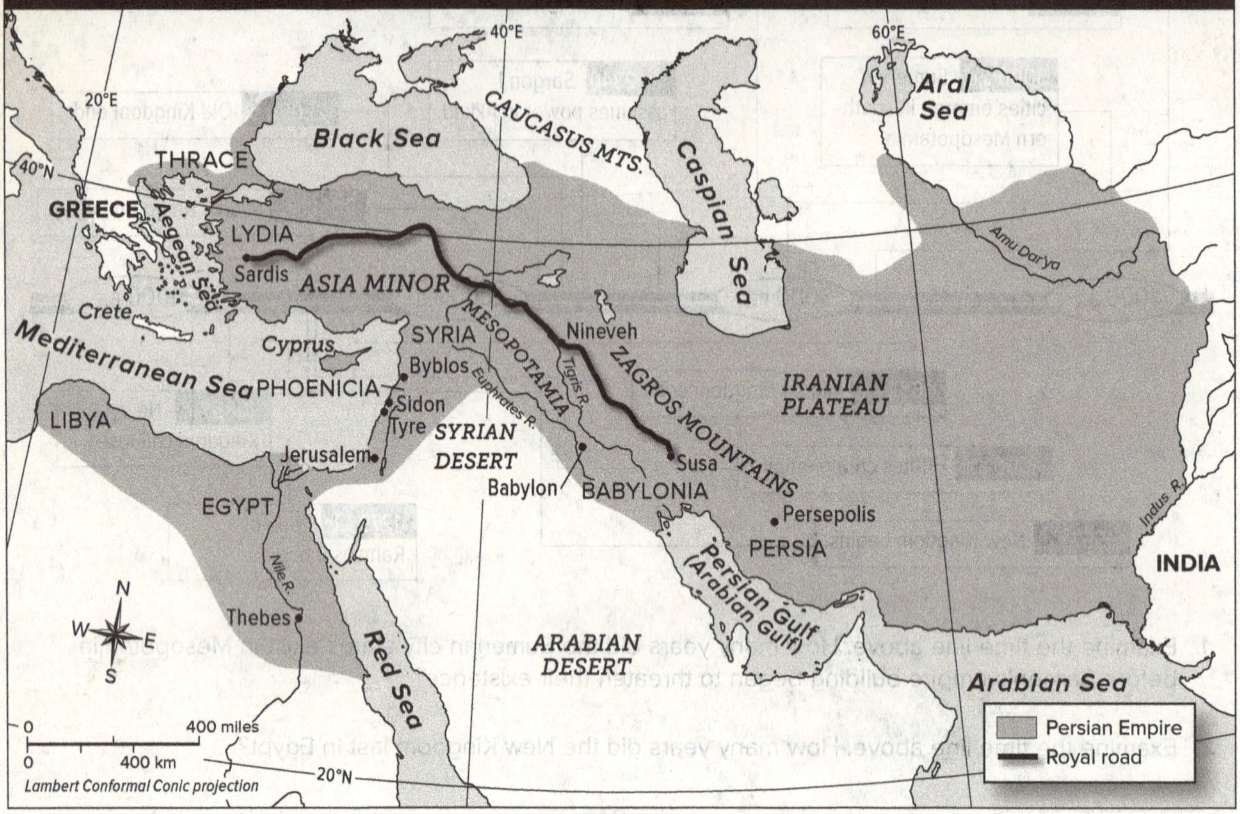

3. Study the map above, which shows the Persian Empire during the reign of Darius. Describe the extent of the Persian Empire at this time.

4. Study the map above, which shows the Persian Empire during the reign of Darius. What does the line marked in red on the map indicate? Why might someone have followed this route?

DIRECTIONS: Essay Answer the following question on a separate piece of paper.

5. After centuries during which independent city-states were the primary political entities in the ancient Near East, rulers appeared who were hungry for bigger conquests and powerful enough to achieve their ambitions. One after another, their great empires rose and fell, but each time important advances were made that improved the administration of large territories. Consider what you have learned from this chapter and use the information to explain the chapter's Enduring Understanding statement: *Strong leaders and militaries established and expanded empires in the ancient Near East, many of which benefited from codified laws, efficient administration, improved communication, and trade.*

NAME ______________________ DATE ______________ CLASS ____________

Lesson Quiz 4-1

networks

The Ancient Greeks

DIRECTIONS: Completion Enter the appropriate word(s) to complete the statement.

1. The poet who wrote the Iliad was named ____________________.

2. The ancient Greeks strove for a kind of ____________________ that they called arête.

3. The Iliad and the Odyssey are examples of ____________________.

4. During the eighth century B.C., the Greeks adopted a new system of writing based on the ____________________.

5. About 80 percent of the geography of Greece is ____________________.

DIRECTIONS: Multiple Choice Indicate the answer choice that best completes the statement or answers the question.

________ **6.** Greek history was influenced by Greece's

A. rivers and deltas.
B. mountains and seacoast.
C. deserts and plains.
D. glaciers and forests.

________ **7.** The teachings of Homer promoted

A. the Phoenician alphabet.
B. agriculture and trade.
C. sailing and warfare.
D. the values of courage, honor, and excellence.

________ **8.** During the Dark Age, some Greeks settled

A. in Crete.
B. on the Indian subcontinent.
C. in Ionia, part of Asia Minor.
D. in Mycenae.

________ **9.** Two major groups that settled within Greece itself were the

A. Aeolians and Dorians.
B. Agamemnons and Homers.
C. Mycenaeans and Minoans.
D. Spartans and the Trojans.

Lesson Quiz 4-2

networks

The Ancient Greeks

DIRECTIONS: Matching Match each item with the correct statement below.

_______ **1.** people captured by the Spartans and forced to work as serfs

_______ **2.** fortified area on a hilltop

_______ **3.** heavily armed foot soldiers

_______ **4.** Athenian reformer who came to power in 594 B.C.

_______ **5.** elected members of Sparta's oligarchy

A. acropolis

B. helots

C. ephors

D. Solon

E. hoplites

DIRECTIONS: Multiple Choice Indicate the answer choice that best completes the statement or answers the question.

_______ **6.** According to one story, a young Spartan warrior was told by his mother to return from the war

A. with lots of black broth.
B. before he turned twenty.
C. in order to serve on the council of elders.
D. either carrying his shield or being carried on it.

_______ **7.** The reforms of Cleisthenes

A. supported tyranny.
B. allowed women to rule.
C. laid the foundations of democracy.
D. freed all the slaves in Athens.

_______ **8.** The word *spartan* has come to mean

A. highly self-disciplined.
B. oligarchical.
C. a lover of literature.
D. democratic.

_______ **9.** The tyrants of ancient Greece were

A. all oppressive and wicked.
B. supporters of aristocrats.
C. rulers who seized power by force.
D. wanted to establish a democratic government.

NAME________________________________ DATE ________________ CLASS __________

Lesson Quiz 4-3

networks

The Ancient Greeks

DIRECTIONS: Modified True/False In the blank, indicate whether the statement is true (T) or false (F). If false edit the statement to make it a true statement.

_______ **1.** According to the legend, the messenger Pheidippides began his twenty-six-mile run in Athens.

_______ **2.** The Persian leader who presented the greatest threat to the Greek empire was named Xerxes.

_______ **3.** The alliance formed by Sparta to help defend Greece from the Persians was called the Delian League.

_______ **4.** During the Age of Pericles, the governing assembly of Athens met every ten days on a hillside east of the Acropolis.

_______ **5.** Pericles spoke about his hopes and ideals for Athens during a public funeral held early in the Peloponnesian War to honor those who had been killed in combat.

DIRECTIONS: Multiple Choice Indicate the answer choice that best completes the statement or answers the question.

_______ **6.** In Athens, during the Age of Pericles, every male citizen

A. was lower class.
B. was eligible to vote on major issues.
C. was in the military.
D. owned slaves.

_______ **7.** After losing the battle of Thermopylae to the Persians, the Athenians

A. abandoned their city.
B. colonized Ionia.
C. fled to Italy.
D. pledged loyalty to Xerxes.

Lesson Quiz 4-4

networks

The Ancient Greeks

DIRECTIONS: Completion Enter the appropriate word(s) to complete the statement.

1. The major gods and goddesses of the Greeks were believed to live on _______________.

2. Socrates' most famous student was named _______________.

3. The most famous building on the Acropolis in Athens is the _______________.

4. One of the subjects that Aristotle wrote about was _______________, or the study of moral principles.

5. The god associated with the most famous oracle in ancient Greece was _______________.

DIRECTIONS: Multiple Choice Indicate the answer choice that best completes the statement or answers the question.

_______ **6.** The ancient Greeks considered religion

A. unnecessary.
B. important only for men.
C. necessary to the well-being of the state.
D. a luxury best left to women.

_______ **7.** Which Greek playwright wrote *Oedipus Rex?*

A. Euripides
B. Aeschylus
C. Sophocles
D. Aristophanes

_______ **8.** According to Plato, a good life can only be achieved if a person

A. lives in a just and rational state.
B. is ruled by a kind and fair monarch.
C. lives a moral and pious life.
D. strictly follows a vegetarian diet.

_______ **9.** The Greek sculptor Polyclitus believed that

A. all sculpture should depict the gods.
B. using proportions and mathematical ratios, the idea human form could be produced.
C. the goal in sculpture was to produce a realistic image.
D. only female artists should sculpt figures of women.

Lesson Quiz 4-5

networks

The Ancient Greeks

DIRECTIONS: Matching Match each item with the correct statement below.

_______ **1.** home of Alexander the Great

_______ **2.** king who conquered the Greeks

_______ **3.** imitating the Greeks

_______ **4.** site of an early battle between the Greeks and the Macedonians

_______ **5.** a writer of comedies during the Hellenistic era

A. Philip II

B. Hellenistic

C. Menander

D. Chaeronea

E. Macedonia

DIRECTIONS: Multiple Choice Indicate the answer choice that best completes the statement or answers the question.

_______ **6.** Which four kingdoms emerged following Alexander the Great's death?

A. Macedonia, Syria, Pergamum, and Egypt
B. Sparta, Rome, Mycenae, and Thebes
C. Persia, Syria, Palestine, and Spain
D. Thermopylae, Marathon, Aegospotami, and Plataea

_______ **7.** According to the philosophy of Epicurus,

A. happiness is the goal of life and can be achieved through the pursuit of pleasure.
B. enlightenment can be achieved only through long periods of meditation.
C. happiness can be found only through the study of poetry.
D. public service will bring about happiness, while selfish pursuits will bring sadness.

_______ **8.** The astronomer Eratosthenes determined that

A. the moon controlled the cyclic rise and fall of the tides.
B. the Earth was at the center of the universe, and the sun rotated around it.
C. the Earth was round, and calculated its circumference, coming within 185 miles (298 kilometers) of the actual figure.
D. the sun was at the center of the universe, and the Earth rotated around it.

_______ **9.** The conquests of Alexander the Great gave rise to the

A. Dark Age, a time when little is known of what happened in Greece.
B. Hellenistic era, during which the Greek language and Greek ideas spread to the non-Greek world.
C. Age of Pericles, when classical Greek ideals were formulated and reached their height.
D. Age of Lawlessness, a period of extreme cruelty and anarchy.

NAME_______________________________ DATE _______________ CLASS __________

Chapter 4 Test, Form A

networks

The Ancient Greeks

DIRECTIONS: Matching Match each item with the correct statement below.

________ **1.** the first Greek civilization	**A.** Age of Pericles
________ **2.** the *Odyssey*, as a type of literature	**B.** Parthenon
________ **3.** Greek city, town, or village and surroundings	**C.** epic poem
________ **4.** important Greek colony city on the Bosporus strait	**D.** oracle
________ **5.** Athenian vote of banishment	**E.** Zeno
________ **6.** height of Athenian power and brilliance	**F.** Mycenae
________ **7.** sacred shrine where priests revealed the future	**G.** ostracism
________ **8.** famous temple to Athena	**H.** Byzantium
________ **9.** founder of Stoicism	**I.** the Hellenistic Era
________ **10.** age that began with Alexander the Great's conquests	**J.** polis

DIRECTIONS: Multiple Choice Indicate the answer choice that best completes the statement or answers the question.

________ **11.** Why did so many different communities with independent ways of life develop in ancient Greece?

A. The mountains in the territory isolated people from one another and prevented different communities from coming together.

B. People came to Greece from many different lands and brought with them their own local customs.

C. The Greeks were naturally very independent minded and tended to settle in communities with others who shared their beliefs.

D. Greek communities were strongly influenced by the ideas of local philosophers, who each promoted different points of view.

NAME________________________________ DATE ______________ CLASS __________

_______ **12.** Scholars continue to debate whether Homer's account of _____ is based on historical fact.

A. a devastating earthquake that destroyed the Mycenaean civilization

B. the sacking of Troy by Mycenaeans under the leadership of King Agamemnon

C. the death of the Athenian runner/messenger Pheidippides

D. King Croesus's encounter with the oracle at Delphi

_______ **13.** The government of Sparta was an oligarchy, which means that it was

A. ruled by a small number of people.

B. ruled by a tyrant.

C. controlled by a popular vote.

D. ruled by a king.

_______ **14.** Why did large numbers of Greeks establish colonies in distant lands between 750 B.C. and 550 B.C.?

A. They were driven out by the tyrants who had seized control of many city-states.

B. They were afraid they would be taken into slavery because they had unpaid debts.

C. The teachings of the philosopher Aristotle encouraged people to leave their homeland.

D. They were seeking a home that was less overpopulated and where they would find fertile farmland.

_______ **15.** According to legend, how did the people in Athens find out what had happened at the battle of Marathon?

A. They went out to the battlefield to watch for themselves.

B. A messenger on horseback rode to Athens with the news.

C. A man named Pheidipiddes ran all the way from the battlefield to Athens.

D. They heard about it when the soldiers returned home from the battle.

_______ **16.** Why did the Athenians stay within their walled city during the Peloponnesian Wars?

A. The Athenians intended to ignore the Spartans' challenge.

B. Pericles knew they were not strong enough to defeat the Spartan army, but he thought the walls could keep them out.

C. The assembly members were still debating how they should respond to the Spartans, so the Athenian army was never ordered to march.

D. They had devised special weaponry that could be deployed from within the city walls against invaders.

_______ **17.** Who said that "the unexamined life is not worth living"?

A. Zeno

B. Aristotle

C. Socrates

D. Euripides

Chapter 4 Test, Form A *cont.*

The Ancient Greeks

_______ **18.** The Athenian dramatist Euripides wrote

A. comedies intended to criticize public figures.

B. a trilogy of tragedies called *The Oresteia*.

C. comedies filled with puns and satire.

D. realistic tragedies that portrayed war as barbaric.

_______ **19.** What was the result of Alexander the Great's conquests?

A. Democracy quickly spread from Greece to a great many lands.

B. Greek language, art, architecture, and literature spread throughout Southeast Asia.

C. After hundreds of years, Persia finally seized control of Greek lands.

D. The progress of Greek scholars and scientists was halted.

_______ **20.** Why, according to legend, did Archimedes run through town shouting "Eureka!"

A. He had established the mathematical constant pi.

B. He had calculated the circumference of the earth.

C. He had experienced a breakthrough in his studies of specific gravity while he was taking a bath.

D. He had discovered the secret to achieving true happiness.

_______ **21.** Herodotus wrote what is considered to be the first

A. novel.

B. tragedy.

C. comedy.

D. real history in Western civilization.

_______ **22.** At its height, Alexander's empire extended as far east as

A. Pakistan.

B. Babylon.

C. Japan.

D. Thebes.

The Ancient Greeks

DIRECTIONS: Short Answer Answer each of the following questions on a separate sheet of paper.

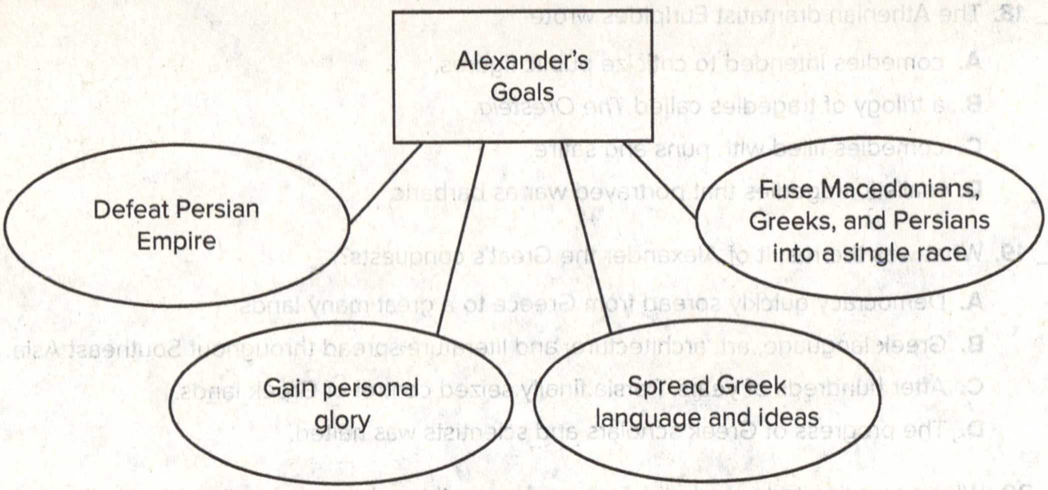

23. Study the graphic organizer above. Using this information and what you have learned from your reading, select two of Alexander's goals and describe how he achieved or failed to achieve each one.

> [A]s soon as they were seven years old they were to be enrolled in certain companies and classes, where they all lived under the same order and discipline, doing their exercises and taking their play together. Of these, he who showed the most conduct and courage was made captain; they had their eyes always upon him, obeyed his orders, and underwent patiently whatsoever punishment he inflicted; so that the whole course of their education was one continued exercise of a ready and perfect obedience.
>
> —Plutarch, *The Lives of Illustrious Men*

24. In the passage above, Plutarch, a biographer who lived in the first and second centuries A.D., is writing about the Spartan culture. Study what he says and consider what you have learned in your other reading. What values of Spartan life does this passage reflect?

NAME________________ DATE__________ CLASS__________

Chapter 4 Test, Form B

networks

The Ancient Greeks

DIRECTIONS: Short Answer Answer each of the following questions on a separate piece of paper.

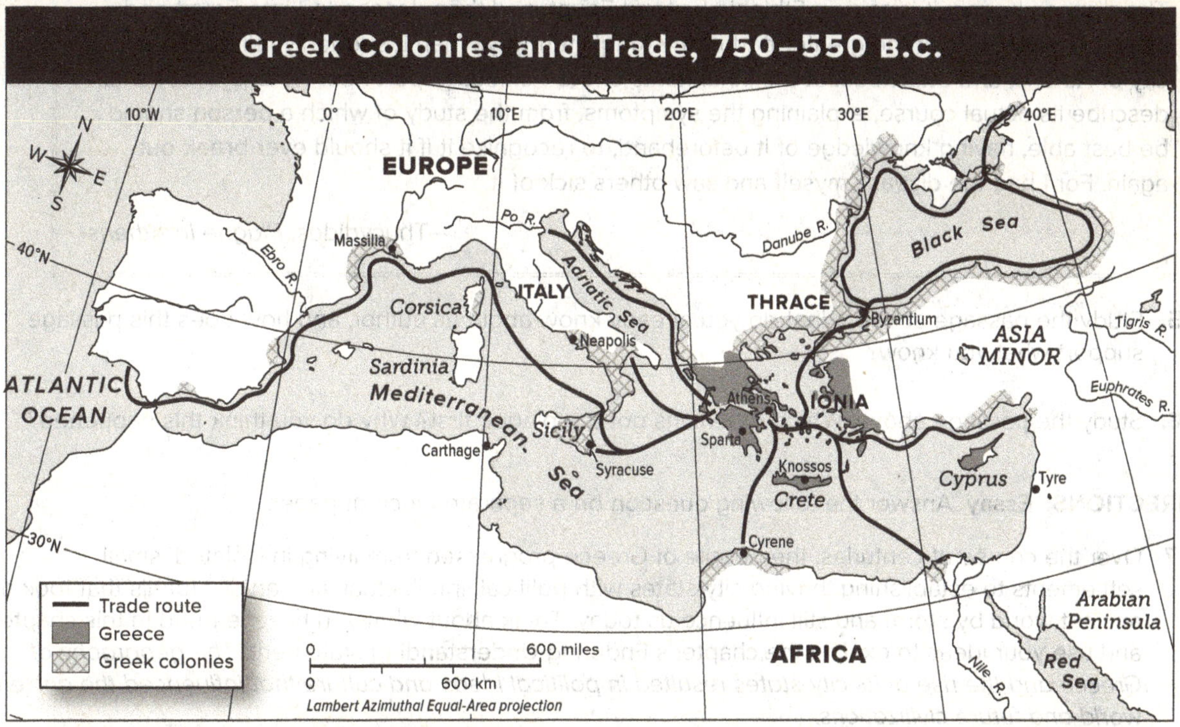

1. Study the map above. What is the easternmost point at which the Greeks established colonies?

2. Study the map above. What connection do you see between the Greek trade routes and the colonies they established during the Dark Age?

> [T]he energy of the intellect is thought to be superior in intensity, because it is contemplative; and to aim at no end beyond itself, and to have a pleasure properly belonging to it; . . . and everything which is attributed to the happy man, evidently exist in this energy; then this must be the perfect happiness of man . . . . But such a life would be better than man could attain to; for he would live thus, not so far forth as he is man, but as there is in him something divine.
>
> —Aristotle

3. Study the text by Aristotle above. What is the main theme of this passage?

4. Study the text by Aristotle above. How does this passage support what you have learned about Aristotle's beliefs?

Chapter 4 Test, Form B *cont.*

The Ancient Greeks

> The disease began, it is said, in Ethiopia beyond Egypt, and then descended into Egypt and Libya and spread over the greater part of the King's territory. Then it suddenly fell upon the city of Athens, and attacked first the inhabitants of the Peirieus [a port near Athens] . . . . I shall describe its actual course, explaining the symptoms, from the study of which a person should be best able, having knowledge of it beforehand, to recognize it if it should ever break out again. For I had the disease myself and saw others sick of it.
>
> —Thucydides, *Plague in Athens*

5. Study the passage above. What do you already know about its author, and how does this passage support what you know?

6. Study the passage above. Which Athenians got the plague first? Why do you think this happened?

DIRECTIONS: Essay Answer the following question on a separate piece of paper.

7. Over the course of centuries, the people of Greece progressed from living in isolated, small settlements to establishing thriving city-states with political, intellectual, and artistic ideals that took the ancient world by storm and still influence us today. Think about what you have learned in this chapter and use your ideas to explain the chapter's Enduring Understanding statement: *The geography of Greece and the rise of its city-states resulted in political ideas and culture that influenced the ancient world and future civilizations.*

NAME_______________________________ DATE ______________ CLASS ___________

Lesson Quiz 5-1

networks

India's First Empires

DIRECTIONS: Matching Match each item with the correct statement below.

1. Term used by the Portuguese to designate the fixed social groups into which individuals are born.

2. followers of this religion believe in a single, universal force called Brahman

3. a method of training developed by the Hindus that is supposed to lead to oneness with Brahman

4. the force generated by a person's actions that determines how the person will be reborn in the next life

5. the word used by Vedic Aryans to refer to the four groups that made up what they viewed as a proper, ordered society.

A. Hinduism

B. karma

C. caste system

D. varnas

E. yoga

DIRECTIONS: Multiple Choice Indicate the answer choice that best completes the statement or answers the question.

_________ **6.** The priestly class of Ancient Indian society were

A. the Vaisyas. **C.** the Brahmins.

B. the Sudras. **D.** the Kshatriyas.

_________ **7.** Reincarnation is the Hindu

A. belief that the individual soul is reborn in a different form.

B. method of training that is supposed to lead to oneness with Brahman.

C. must worship the leader as a god.

D. of a woman is superior.

_________ **8.** Brahma the Creator, Vishnu the Preserver, and Shiva the Destroyer are the three chief

A. leaders of Ancient India.

B. humanlike gods in Hinduism.

C. Aryan warriors whose actions illustrate the importance of duty.

D. characters in the Bhagavad Gita, India's great religious poem.

_________ **9.** The lowest level of Ancient Indian society who were given tasks seen as the most polluting, such as collecting trash and handling dead bodies, were

A. the Brahmins. **C.** *dalit*

B. the Vaisyas. **D.** the Kshatriyas.

NAME________________________________ DATE __________________ CLASS __________

Lesson Quiz 5-2

networks

India's First Empires

DIRECTIONS: Matching Match each item with the correct statement below.

1. eight steps that Buddhists follow on the path to enlightenment

2. self-denial as a method to achieve an understanding of ultimate reality

3. ultimate reality, or the end of the self and a reunion with the Great World Soul

4. Siddhārtha Gautama's message about suffering and desire

5. the "Enlightened One"

A. nirvana
B. the Four Noble Truths
C. asceticism
D. Buddha
E. Middle Path

DIRECTIONS: Multiple Choice Indicate the answer choice that best completes the statement or answers the question.

________ **6.** Siddhārtha Gautama was the founder of

A. Hinduism.
B. Buddhism.
C. the caste system.
D. the holy city of Varanasi.

________ **7.** One way that Buddhism differed from Hinduism was Buddhists believed that

A. women were the equals of men.
B. the material world held the key to happiness.
C. people should be responsible for their own lives.
D. self-denial is necessary to achieve an understanding of ultimate reality.

________ **8.** Another way that Buddhism differed from Hinduism was that Buddhists rejected

A. the many Hindu gods.
B. the idea of awakening.
C. the simplicity of Hinduism.
D. the five precepts of right action.

________ **9.** The Eightfold Path includes the idea that we must

A. trust our senses over our minds.
B. worship images of the Buddha.
C. do work that uplifts our being.
D. disregard the Four Noble Truths.

NAME______________________ DATE ______________ CLASS __________

Lesson Quiz 5-3

networks

India's First Empires

DIRECTIONS: Matching Match each item with the correct statement below.

1. type of religious structure originally meant to house relics of the Buddha

2. famous Indian mathematician and one of the first scientists known to have used algebra

3. India's golden age of culture flourished under this monarch

4. the greatest ruler in Indian history

5. a literary work about the fictional ruler Rama

A. Aśoka

B. the Ramayana

C. Aryabhata

D. stupa

E. Candra Gupta II

DIRECTIONS: Multiple Choice Indicate the answer choice that best completes the statement or answers the question.

________ **6.** After the collapse of the Mauryan Empire, the people who spread over northern India as far as the central Ganges Valley into modern-day Pakistan, Afghanistan, and Central Asia were the

A. Arabs.

B. Guptas.

C. Kushans.

D. Persians.

________ **7.** Gupta rulers earned large profits from

A. agriculture.

B. fishing.

C. literary works.

D. religious trade.

________ **8.** During his reign, Aśoka

A. cut down trees along roads.

B. sponsored Hindu missionaries.

C. set up hospitals for people and animals.

D. prohibited trade with China and the Mediterranean.

________ **9.** The Kushans adapted

A. the Greek alphabet.

B. a calendar based on the sun and moon.

C. Kalasindra's poem *The Cloud Messenger*.

D. the Arabic numerical system.

NAME ______________ DATE ______________ CLASS ______________

Chapter 5 Test, Form A

networks

India's First Empires

DIRECTIONS: Matching Match each item with the correct statement below.

_____ **1.** the warrior-administrator class in Indian society

_____ **2.** different cultures shaped this empire because a section of the Silk Road passed through it

_____ **3.** In Hinduism, the divine law that requires karma and requires all people to do their duty based on their status in society

_____ **4.** religion that claims all people can achieve nirvana

_____ **5.** longest poem in any written language

_____ **6.** religion that reveres the cow as sacred and whose goal is to achieve ultimate reality with a single universal force

_____ **7.** one of three chief human-like gods in the Hindu religion

_____ **8.** belief that the soul is reborn after death

_____ **9.** determined the type of job people could have, whom they could marry, and with whom they could socialize

_____ **10.** prosperous cities rose along the main trade routes throughout India during this empire

A. reincarnation

B. caste

C. *Mahabharata*

D. Shiva the Destroyer

E. Buddhism

F. Kshatriyas

G. Gupta

H. Hinduism

I. dharma

J. Kushan

DIRECTIONS: Multiple Choice Indicate the answer choice that best completes the statement or answers the question.

_____ **11.** Which empire traded with China, Southeast Asia, and the Mediterranean?

A. the Gupta Empire

B. the Persian Kingdom

C. the Mauryan Dynasty

D. the Aryan Empire

_____ **12.** Who was Siddhārtha Gautama?

A. ruler of the Aryans

B. founder of Buddhism

C. ruler of the Mauryans

D. king of the Guptas

_______ **13.** The Brahmins, Kshatriyas, Vaisyas, and Sudras were four divisions of ancient Indian society known as

A. yoga.

B. kharma.

C. dharma.

D. varnas.

_______ **14.** The golden age of Indian culture occurred under the

A. Mauryan Empire.

B. Gupta Empire.

C. Kushan Empire.

D. Aryan Empire.

_______ **15.** Ancient Indians excelled in the science of

A. biology.

B. chemistry.

C. physics.

D. astronomy.

_______ **16.** Who believed that the physical surroundings of humans—the material world—were simply illusions?

A. Asoka

B. Candra Gupta II

C. Siddhārtha Gautama

D. Candragupta Maurya

_______ **17.** Buddhists believe that it is possible to reach enlightenment by

A. practicing self-denial.

B. worshipping the gods.

C. rejecting the concept of reincarnation.

D. following the Middle Path, known as the Eightfold Path.

Chapter 5 Test, Form A *cont.*

networks

India's First Empires

_______ **18.** A distinct feature of the Kushan Empire was the development of

A. a calendar.
B. hospitals.
C. algebra.
D. stone pillars.

_______ **19.** A common belief shared by Hindus and Buddhists is that

A. humans can merge with a single universal force.
B. there are many gods with human-like characteristics.
C. all we are is the result of what we have thought.
D. the way to end desire is to follow the Middle Path.

_______ **20.** A person's caste was difficult to escape because it was based on

A. ideas about wealth.
B. the practice of yoga.
C. the Bhagavad Gita.
D. beliefs about religious purity.

_______ **21.** Herodotus wrote what is considered to be the first

A. novel.
B. tragedy.
C. comedy.
D. real history in Western civilization.

_______ **22.** At its height, Alexander's empire extended as far east as

A. Pakistan.
B. Babylon.
C. Japan.
D. Thebes.

Chapter 5 Test, Form A *cont.*

networks

India's First Empires

DIRECTIONS: Short Answer Answer each of the following questions.

For India is a land of exceptional beauty, and since it is crossed by many rivers it is supplied with water over its whole area and produces two harvests each year. As a result it has such an abundance of the necessities of life that at all times it blesses its inhabitants with plentiful enjoyment of them. People say that because of the favorable climate in those parts the country has never endured famine or the destruction of crops. Also, it has an unbelievable profusion of elephants, which both in courage and bodily strength far surpass those of Libya, and likewise gold, silver, iron and copper; further, one can find within its borders great quantities of precious stones of every kind and of almost all other objects which contribute to luxury and wealth.

—Diodorus Siculus, a Greek historian writing in the first century B.C., quoted in *The Making of Roman India*

23. Note the features of India that Diodorus Siculus describes. How might these features effect India's ability to flourish as a great empire?

____

____

____

____

____

By order of the Beloved of the Gods [Aoeoka]. Addressed to the officers in charge...Let us win the affection of all men. All men are my children, and as I wish all welfare and happiness in this world and the rest for my own children, so do I wish it for all men. ...For that purpose many officials are employed among the people to instruct them in righteousness and to explain it to them.

—quoted in *Aoeoka Maurya,* 1966

24. How do Aoeoka's words reflect some of the principles of Buddhism?

____

____

____

____

____

Chapter 5 Test, Form B

India's First Empires

DIRECTIONS: Short Answer Answer each of the following questions on a separate piece of paper.

Number Systems Based on 10

The number system used most widely today was likely invented by the Hindus. This system, based on 10 numbers, was adopted by the Arab empires and probably reached Europe around the tenth century. However, it was some time before this system replaced the Roman numerals then in use. Number systems do not have to be based on 10 numbers. The ancient Babylonians, for example, based their system on 60 numbers.

Babylonian	𒁹	𒈫	𒐈	𒐉	𒐊	𒐋	𒑂	𒑄	𒑆	𒌋	
Egyptian	I	II	III	IIII	IIIII	IIIIII	IIIIIII	IIIIIIII	IIIIIIIII	∩	
Greek	A	B	Γ	Δ	E	F	Z	H	Θ	I	
Roman	I	II	III	IV	V	VI	VII	VIII	IX	X	
Ancient Chinese	一	二	三	四	五	六	七	八	九	十	
Mayan	𝋡	𝋢	𝋣	𝋤	𝋥	𝋦	𝋧	𝋨	𝋩	𝋪	𝋠
Hindu	१	२	३	४	५	६	७	८	९	१०	०
15th-Century Arabic/European	1	2	3	4	5	6	7	8	9	10	0
Modern Arabic/European	1	2	3	4	5	6	7	8	9	10	0

1. Read the information on the chart and study the various number systems. Which number system is used most widely today? In which culture did the number system that is most widely used today originate?

2. Which number systems included a symbol that represented the number zero?

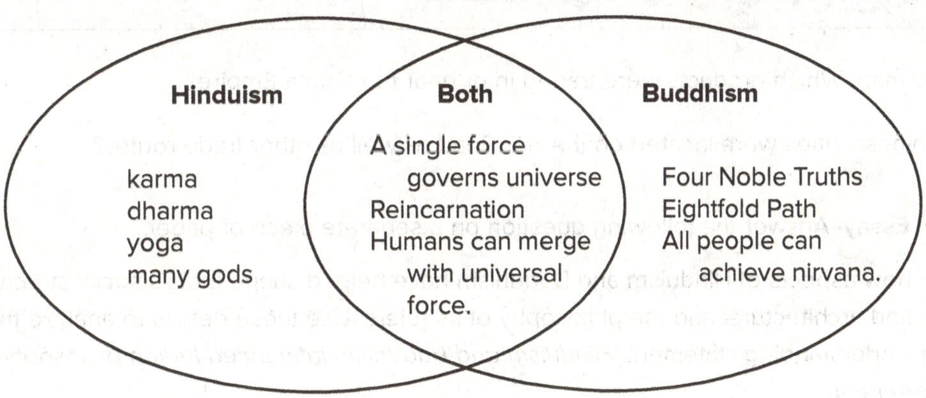

3. According to the Venn diagram above, what might the future hold for a Buddhist?

4. Which religion claims that humans can merge with a universal force?

Chapter 5 Test, Form B *cont.*

networks

India's First Empires

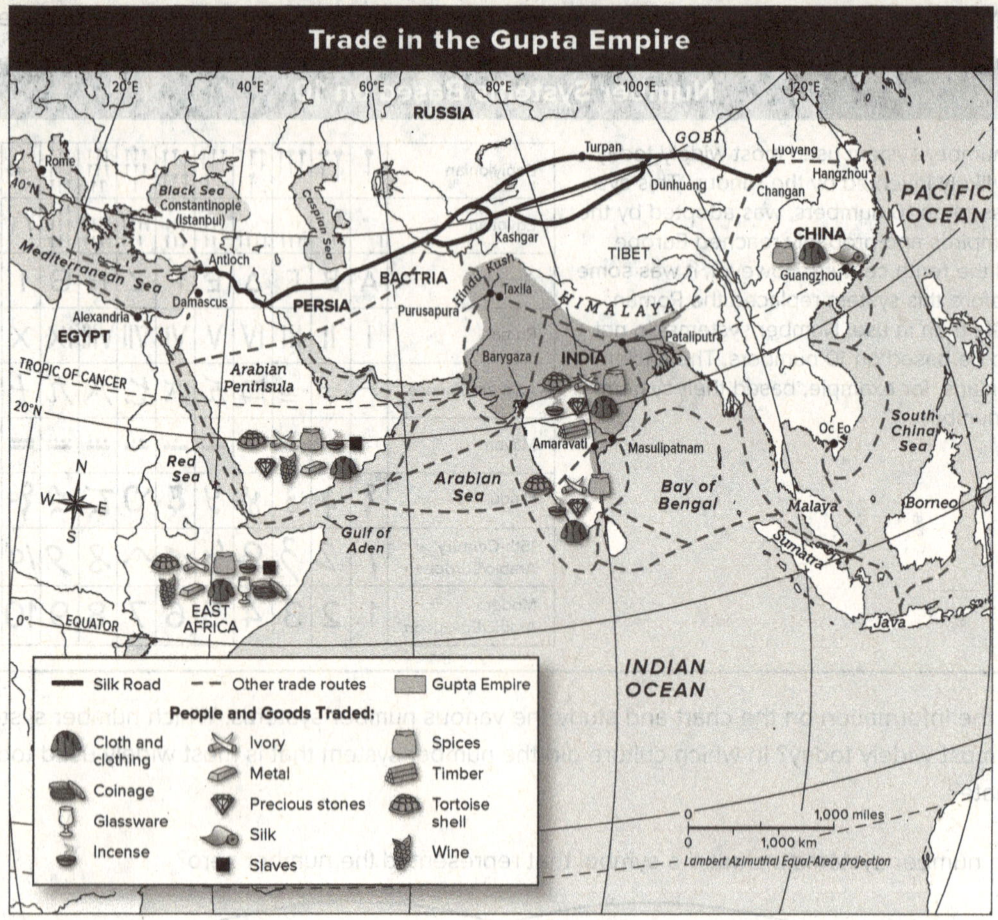

5. Study the map. Which products were traded in or near the Gupta Empire?

6. Which Chinese cities were located on the Silk Road as well as other trade routes?

DIRECTIONS: Essay Answer the following question on a separate piece of paper.

7. Consider how aspects of Hinduism and Buddhism have helped shape India's social structure, its literature and architecture, and the philosophy of its rulers. Use these details to analyze the chapter's Enduring Understanding statement: *Hinduism and Buddhism influenced Indian philosophies, culture, and government.*

NAME ______________________ DATE ______________ CLASS __________

Lesson Quiz 6-1

networks

The First Chinese Empires

DIRECTIONS: Completion Enter the appropriate word(s) to complete the statement.

1. The followers of Confucius recorded his sayings in the ____________________.

2. Daoism sets forth proper forms of ____________________.

3. Confucius believed that the early ____________________ was a golden age, when "the world was shared by all alike."

4. The relationships between parents and children, husbands and wives, siblings, friends, and rulers and their subjects are the ____________________ Relationships.

5. Duty and ____________________ are two elements of the Confucian view of the Dao.

DIRECTIONS: Multiple Choice Indicate the answer choice that best completes the statement or answers the question.

_______ **6.** Which of the following statements about Confucianism, Daoism, and Legalism is true?

A. They all seek to understand humanity's relationship with the divine.
B. All three philosophies assume that people are essentially good.
C. They are primarily concerned with the material world and social stability.
D. All three philosophies preach the value of working hard.

_______ **7.** The Legalists believed that a strong ruler was needed to

A. support Daoism.
B. keep order.
C. maintain good trade relations.
D. show compassion.

_______ **8.** According to Confucius, what is the "foundation, whence all other virtues spring"?

A. the duty of children to revere their parents
B. an understanding of the spiritual world
C. the willingness to work hard and get an education
D. being from an aristocratic family

_______ **9.** The words "The universe is sacred. You cannot improve it. If you try to change it, you will ruin it." reflect the beliefs of which philosophy?

A. Confucianism
B. Daoism
C. Legalism
D. ethics

_______ **10.** Why did the Legalists advocate harsh laws and stiff punishments?

A. That was the best way to ensure that "superior men" would rise to the top.
B. Those were the only laws that could be administered fairly.
C. They wanted strong laws so that the ruler would be free to show compassion.
D. They believed people we not capable of being good.

NAME_______________________ DATE_____________ CLASS_________

Lesson Quiz 6-2

networks

The First Chinese Empires

DIRECTIONS: Modified True/False In the blank, indicate whether the statement is true (T) or false (F). If false edit the statement to make it a true statement.

_________ **1.** Qin Shihuangdi initiated the building of the Wall of Ten Thousand *Li* to block invaders from the south.

____

____

_________ **2.** To make each terra-cotta soldier unique, 10 different head shapes were used and then finished by hand.

____

____

_________ **3.** After the death of Qin Shihuangdi, his son ruled the empire.

____

____

_________ **4.** Qin Shihuangdi ruled according to the principles of Confucianism.

____

____

_________ **5.** Qin Shihuangdi created a single currency in his empire.

____

____

DIRECTIONS: Multiple Choice Indicate the answer choice that best completes the statement or answers the question.

_________ **6.** How was the central bureaucracy of the Qin dynasty organized?

A. There were 4 divisions: judicial, military, religious, and agricultural.

B. There were 3 divisions: civil, military, and censorate.

C. There were 2 divisions: one for the urban areas and one for the rural areas.

D. There were 5 divisions: one for each of the five provinces.

_________ **7.** How did Qin Shihuangdi eliminate rivals and gain an important tax base?

A. He made wealthy families pay a bribe so that their sons could have jobs.

B. He put his soldiers on the roads between the estates of wealthy landowners and made them pay heavy tolls to travel on them.

C. He seized the estates of wealthy landowners and gave the lands to the peasants; he then taxed the peasants.

D. He forced all the sons of wealthy landowners to join his army but allowed their families to pay large bribes to get them out of military service.

NAME_______________ DATE _______________ CLASS _______________

Lesson Quiz 6-3

networks

The First Chinese Empires

DIRECTIONS: Matching Match each item with the correct statement below.

_______ **1.** helped enable Chinese trade in Southeast Asia and India

_______ **2.** added the territory south of the Chang Jiang to the empire

_______ **3.** led to the invention of steel

_______ **4.** wrote biographies that combined political and social history

_______ **5.** was not made in Europe until the twelfth century

A. Han Wudi

B. Ban Gu

C. rudder

D. paper

E. iron casting

DIRECTIONS: Multiple Choice Indicate the answer choice that best completes the statement or answers the question.

_______ **6.** Which of the following was a factor in peasant uprisings in the late Han dynasty?

A. the difficulty of civil service examinations
B. the Han government's emphasis on the teachings of Confucius
C. concentration of land in the hands of the wealthy
D. invasions by nomadic tribes from the north

_______ **7.** What was the effect of the technical advancements in the Han dynasty?

A. national self-sufficiency that led to a decrease in trade
B. more people with free time to study religion
C. a general decrease in economic prosperity
D. a general increase in economic prosperity

_______ **8.** At the end of the Han dynasty in A.D. 221, the population of China had

A. stayed the same as it had been in A.D. 2.
B. decreased by 40 million since A.D. 2.
C. decreased by 10 million since A.D. 2.
D. increased by 40 million since A.D. 2.

_______ **9.** How were government officials chosen in the Han dynasty?

A. by birth
B. by military service
C. by a competitive examination
D. by lottery

Chapter 6 Test, Form A

networks

The First Chinese Empires

DIRECTIONS: Matching Match each item with the correct statement below.

_______ **1.** proposed that human beings were evil by nature

_______ **2.** expanded the Chinese Empire into what is now Vietnam

_______ **3.** "Way"

_______ **4.** papermaking was invented during this dynasty

_______ **5.** system of ideas based on the teachings of "Master Kung"

_______ **6.** checked on government officials to make sure they were doing their jobs

_______ **7.** used the principles of Legalism to govern

_______ **8.** system of ideas based on Laozi's teachings

_______ **9.** administrative offices of a government which are awarded based on a competitive exam

_______ **10.** built "The Wall of Ten Thousand *Li*"

A. Daoism

B. Confucianism

C. Legalism

D. Qin Shihuangdi

E. Han Wudi

F. civil service

G. censorate

H. Dao

I. Qin

J. Han

DIRECTIONS: Multiple Choice Indicate the answer choice that best completes the statement or answers the question.

_______ **11.** Harmony with nature and the universal order are beliefs of

A. Daoism.

B. Confucianism.

C. Zoroastrianism.

D. the Legalists.

_______ **12.** An important concept that became a crucial part of Chinese history was

A. the view that art, poetry, and literature were important to soldiers.

B. the Confucian belief that the government should be open to all men of superior talent.

C. the belief that the Great Wall would protect China from all enemies.

D. the Shaolin view that one must be able to do combat mentally as well as physically.

_______ **13.** One of the technological advances of the Han dynasty was

A. the umbrella.

B. the invention of water mills for grinding grain.

C. a decimal system of counting in tens, which is still used today.

D. the first permanent marker.

_______ **14.** The first Han emperor discarded

A. communism for socialism.

B. Daoism and adopted Legalism.

C. Legalism and adopted Confucianism.

D. all religion.

_______ **15.** The founder of the Han dynasty was

A. Liu Pang, a man of peasant origin.

B. Qin Shihuangdi, who began a program of intense rice cultivation.

C. Zhou Shang, who claimed to have the Mandate of Heaven.

D. Han Wudi, who added the southern regions of Persia to the empire.

_______ **16.** The invention that led to major expansion of trade in the Han period was

A. the technology of papermaking.

B. the process for developing rubber.

C. textile manufacturing.

D. the development of fore-and-aft rigging and rudders on ships.

_______ **17.** In 1974 farmers digging a well about 35 miles east of Xian discovered

A. a water mill.

B. an army of terra-cotta warriors.

C. the ruins of a Xiongnu temple.

D. the lost city of Beijing.

_______ **18.** The system of walls linked by Qin Shihuangdi became

A. the civil division.

B. terra cotta.

C. the military division.

D. the Great Wall of China.

_______ **19.** The Qin and Han dynasties both

A. had strong central governments.

B. established religions.

C. started civil wars.

D. chose officials by birth.

_______ **20.** Confucius believed that people should be governed by

A. harsh laws and strict punishments.

B. harmony with nature.

C. the Mandate of Heaven.

D. the Five Constant Relationships.

_______ **21.** Why did the Legalists advocate harsh laws and stiff punishments for keeping public order?

A. That was the best way to ensure that "superior men" would rise to the top.

B. Those were the only laws that could be administered fairly.

C. They wanted strong laws so that the ruler would be free to show compassion.

D. They believed people we not capable of being good.

_______ **22.** Which of the following territories were added to the empire during the Han dynasty?

A. parts of Central Asia

B. parts of India

C. Xianyang

D. Xiongnu

Chapter 6 Test, Form A *cont.*

networks

The First Chinese Empires

DIRECTIONS: Short Answer Answer each of the following questions.

23. Describe the impact of the Han period on Chinese free peasants.

24. Describe the ways in which the two elements of duty and humanity were expressed in the Confucian view of the Dao. Explain how Confucius believed those elements should be reflected in the relationship between a ruler and his people.

> The reason they did not dare exert their loyalty and correct the errors of the ruler was the Qin's customs forbade the mentioning of inauspicious matters. Before their words of loyal advice were even out of their mouths, they would have been condemned to execution. This insured that men of the empire would incline their ears to listen, stand in an attitude of solemn attention, but clamp their mouths shut and never speak out.
>
> —Sima Qian, *Records of the Grand Historian*

25. The quote above describes one reason for the decline of the Qin dynasty. Based on your reading of the chapter, what factors do you think were responsible for that decline?

Chapter 6 Test, Form B

networks

The First Chinese Empires

DIRECTIONS: Short Answer Answer each of the following questions on a separate piece of paper.

Putting a value on status
will cause people to compete....
Thus the Sage rules
by stilling minds and opening hearts
by filling bellies and strengthening bones
He shows people how to be simple
and live without desires
To be content
and not look for other ways....
When action is pure and selfless
Everything settles into its own perfect place

—*Verse 3, Tao Te Ching*

1. How does the quote above reflect what you have learned about the principles of Daoism?

2. How does the philosophy expressed in the quote above differ from the philosophy of Confucianism?

3. How does the philosophy expressed in the quote above differ from the philosophy of Legalism?

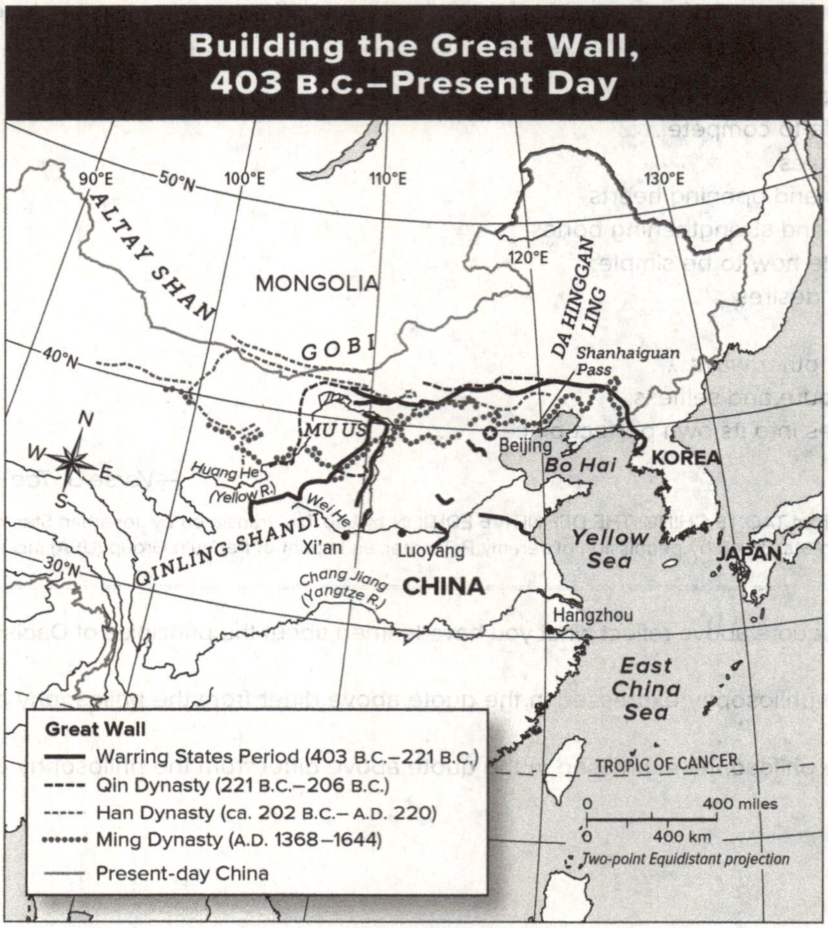

4. Using the legend provided with the map above, give an approximate measure of the length of the Great Wall.

5. Using the information from the map, which dynasty contributed the most to the Great Wall? Why did China begin constructing this wall?

DIRECTIONS: Essay Answer the following question on a separate piece of paper.

6. As a unified China emerged from a period of chaos and civil war, new ideas were developed to determine the best way to rule this new empire. Use the content taught in this chapter to explain the chapter's Enduring Understanding statement: *During the Qin and Han dynasties, all aspects of Chinese culture were permeated by the philosophies of Legalism, Daoism, and Confucianism, which sought order and balance in society.*

NAME _______________________ DATE _____________ CLASS _____________

Lesson Quiz 7-1

networks

The Romans

DIRECTIONS: Modified True/False In the blank, indicate whether the statement is true (T) or false (F). If false edit the statement to make it a true statement.

_______ **1.** Rome's location and its distance from the sea encouraged attacks by pirates.

____

____

_______ **2.** Unlike Greece, Italy's limited farmland prevented Rome from expanding.

____

____

_______ **3.** The Etruscans, from whom the Romans borrowed their style of dress, heavily influenced early Romans.

____

____

_______ **4.** There was little conflict between the plebeians and the patricians, the two main social and political groups in Rome.

____

____

_______ **5.** After the conquest of the Italian peninsula, Rome fought the Etruscans for control of the Mediterranean.

____

____

DIRECTIONS: Multiple Choice Indicate the answer choice that best completes the statement or answers the question.

_______ **6.** What advantage did Rome's location on the Tiber River provide?

A. access to the sea
B. contact with pirates
C. large plots of land
D. fertile plains

_______ **7.** The conflict between the plebeians and the patricians was known as the

A. Law of the Nations.
B. Second Punic War.
C. council of the plebs.
D. struggle of the orders.

_______ **8.** The Roman Senate was a select group of

A. patricians.
B. consuls.
C. praetors.
D. emperors.

NAME_______________________________________ DATE ________________ CLASS ____________

Lesson Quiz 7-2

networks

The Romans

DIRECTIONS: Matching Match each item with the correct statement below.

________ **1.** Roman general who created a new recruitment system

________ **2.** group composed of Caesar, Crassus, and Pompey

________ **3.** Rome's first emperor

________ **4.** men who tried to return land to small farmers

________ **5.** dictator who rose to power in 47 B.C.

A. Gracchus brothers

B. First Triumvirate

C. Julius Caesar

D. Marius

E. Augustus

DIRECTIONS: Multiple Choice Indicate the answer choice that best completes the statement or answers the question.

________ **6.** What was a product of Tiberius and Gaius Gracchus's attempted reforms?

A. instability and the assassination of Tiberius and Gaius
B. the election of both Tiberius and Gaius to the Roman Senate
C. the destruction of the First Triumvirate
D. growth of a new class of wealthy plebeians

________ **7.** Sulla's seizure of Rome in 82 B.C. was partly the legacy of

A. Caesar's assassination in the senate.
B. a new military recruitment system.
C. Augustus's defeat of Antony.
D. the fall of the Second Triumvirate.

________ **8.** Julius Caesar sparked a civil war that led to his dictatorship by crossing the

A. Tiber.
B. Po.
C. Appenine.
D. Rubicon.

________ **9.** In 31 B.C., Octavian defeated the army and navy of

A. Lucius Cornelius Sulla.
B. Antony and Cleopatra.
C. Pompey and Crassus.
D. Lepidus and Caesar.

NAME______________________ DATE ______________ CLASS ____________

Lesson Quiz 7-3

networks

The Romans

DIRECTIONS: Completion Enter the appropriate word(s) to complete the statement.

1. Beginning in the second century and lasting for nearly 200 years, the ____________________ represented a period of stability and many public works projects.

2. Prosperity in the Early Empire led to much trade, including trade with ____________________, which provided the empire with silk goods.

3. The greatest poet of the Augustan age was ____________________, author of the Aeneid.

4. The heart of Roman society was the family, which was headed by the ____________________.

5. Romans adopted many aspects of the ____________________ style of art.

DIRECTIONS: Multiple Choice Indicate the answer choice that best completes the statement or answers the question.

_______ 6. The *Pax Romana* was a

A. period of peace and prosperity.
B. leader of the senate.
C. series of fortifications.
D. program of public works.

_______ 7. While the emperors created a sense of unity throughout the empire, they also

A. outlawed non-Roman religions.
B. denied citizenship to provincials.
C. allowed competing emperors.
D. respected many local customs.

_______ 8. What allowed Romans to construct massive, though stable, buildings?

A. arches
B. concrete
C. slave labor
D. aqueducts

_______ 9. Although the city of Rome was magnificent and wealthy,

A. very few citizens chose to live there.
B. its public buildings were poorly built.
C. conditions for the poor were terrible.
D. it provided few entertainments.

_______ 10. Which best describes a key feature of Rome's official state religion?

A. Romans worshipped gods and goddesses.
B. Romans believed in only one god.
C. Augustus outlawed religious displays.
D. Emperors were never worshipped as gods.

Chapter 7 Test, Form A

networks

The Romans

DIRECTIONS: Matching Match each item with the correct statement below.

_____ **1.** the shared rule of Julius Caesar, Crassus, and Pompey

_____ **2.** commander in chief

_____ **3.** author of the Aeneid

_____ **4.** dominant male head of family

_____ **5.** group of craftsmen, merchants, and small farmers

_____ **6.** often dangerous apartments for the poor

_____ **7.** chief executive of the Roman Republic

_____ **8.** great landowners, ruling class

_____ **9.** official in chare of enforcing civil law

_____ **10.** Carthaginian general

A. Hannibal

B. plebeian

C. praetor

D. patrician

E. consul

F. First Triumvirate

G. Virgil

H. imperator

I. paterfamilias

J. *insulae*

DIRECTIONS: Multiple Choice Indicate the answer choice that best completes the statement or answers the question.

_____ **11.** The Appenine Mountains

A. split Rome into many small villages.

B. kept Rome from interacting with the Etruscans.

C. did not prevent expansion of the city.

D. protected Rome from the Greeks.

_____ **12.** From which group did the Romans borrow their style of dress?

A. Greeks

B. Etruscans

C. Carthaginians

D. Gauls

_______ **13.** Who attempted to redistribute land to the poor with disastrous results?

A. Tiberius and Gaius Gracchus
B. Lucius Cornelius Sulla
C. Julius Caesar and Crassus
D. Pompey and Caesar Augustus

_______ **14.** Marius changed Rome's military recruitment system by

A. making recruits swear an imperial oath.
B. accepting patrician recruits.
C. recruiting the landless poor.
D. accepting non-Roman recruits.

_______ **15.** In 53 B.C., the First Triumvirate ended with the death of

A. Julius Caesar.
B. Octavian.
C. Pompey.
D. Crassus.

_______ **16.** Who was appointed dictator after defeating Pompey?

A. Julius Caesar
B. Octavian
C. Antony
D. Crassus

_______ **17.** After the Second Triumvirate, with whom did Antony war for control of Rome?

A. Julius Caesar
B. Octavian
C. Lepidus
D. Crassus

________ **18.** Caesar Augustus changed the way the provinces were ruled by

A. making all free people citizens of Rome.

B. preventing senatorial interference.

C. removing his armies from the provinces.

D. choosing the leaders of those provinces.

________ **19.** *Pax Romana*, a long period of peace, ushered in

A. large-scale building programs.

B. a decline in imperial power.

C. the reign of Nero.

D. the end of external trade.

________ **20.** Which of the following was an action taken by Emperor Caracalla?

A. bringing an end to imperial taxation

B. building a wall to prevent invasion

C. granting citizenship to all free people

D. reducing provincial building programs

________ **21.** Which describes one of Augustus's reforms?

A. He returned all power to the Roman people.

B. The senate was completely disbanded.

C. Governors were to be chosen by emperors.

D. The size of the senate was reduced.

DIRECTIONS: Short Answer Answer each of the following questions.

22. Based on your understanding of the early Roman Empire, why was trade vital to the period known as *Pax Romana?*

> But nowadays, with no vote . . . , their motto is 'Couldn't care less.' Time was when their vote elected generals, heads of state, commanders of legions: but now . . . there's only two things that concern them: Bread and Circuses.
>
> —The poet Juvenal

23. What does Juvenal suggest about the effects of empire on everyday Roman citizens? What other factors may have affected the attitudes of these citizens?

____

____

____

____

24. How do you think Rome's religious practices and its citizens' tolerance of other religions aided the expansion and preservation of the empire?

____

____

____

____

NAME ______________________ DATE ____________ CLASS ____________

Chapter 7 Test, Form B

networks

The Romans

DIRECTIONS: Short Answer Answer each of the following questions below.

Greek God	Roman God	Role
Ares	Mars	god of war
Zeus	Jupiter	chief god
Hera	Juna	wife of chief god
Aphrodite	Venus	goddess of love
Artemis	Diana	goddess of the hunt
Athena	Minerva	goddess of wisdom
Hermes	Mercury	messenger god
Hades	Pluto	god of the underworld
Poseidon	Neptune	god of the sea
Hephaestus	Vulcan	god of fire

1. According to this chart who was the Greek god of the underworld? What name did the Romans give to this god?

____

____

2. What does this chart suggest about the cultural relationship between the Greeks and the Romans?

____

____

> In great buildings as well as in other things the rest of the world has been outdone by us Romans. If, indeed, all the buildings in our City are considered in the aggregate, and supposing them—so to say—all thrown together in one vast mass, the united grandeur of them would lead one to imagine that we were describing another world, accumulated in a single spot.
>
> —Pliny the Elder, from *Natural History,* c. 79 A.D.

3. According to Pliny the Elder, in what way had Rome surpassed all other nations?

____

____

NAME ______________________ DATE ______________ CLASS ______________

Chapter 7 Test, Form B *cont.*

The Romans

4. What factors contributed to Rome's ability to surpass the world in this way?

____

____

> For other peoples will, I do not doubt,
> still cast their bronze to breathe with softer features,
> or draw out of the marble living lines,
> plead causes better, trace the ways of heaven
> with wands and tell the rising constellations;
> but yours will be the rulership of nations,
> remember, Roman, these will be your arts:
> to teach the ways of peace to those you conquer,
> to spare defeated peoples, tame the proud.
>
> —Virgil, *The Aeneid*, Book VI, lines 847–53

5. According to Virgil, what is the medium of Romans?

____

____

6. Although Virgil may disagree, in what other fields did the Romans excel?

____

____

DIRECTIONS: Essay Answer the following question on a separate piece of paper.

7. The Roman Republic and the early period of the Roman Empire were marked by internal and external conflicts and a vast expansion of political, cultural, and economic power. Use the information presented in this chapter to explain the chapter's Enduring Understanding statement: *During its republic and early empire, Rome gradually conquered, controlled, and influenced the culture of the entire Mediterranean world.*

NAME_______________________ DATE ____________ CLASS ________

Lesson Quiz 8-1

networks

The Byzantine Empire and Emerging Europe

DIRECTIONS: Matching Match each item with the correct statement below.

_______ **1.** second part of the Christian Bible

_______ **2.** a Roman official in charge of a province

_______ **3.** first Christian emperor

_______ **4.** "anointed one"

_______ **5.** church leaders

A. Constantine

B. clergy

C. *Christos*

D. New Testament

E. procurator

DIRECTIONS: Multiple Choice Indicate the answer choice that best completes the statement or answers the question.

_______ **6.** The _______________ were a group of Jews who called for the violent overthrow of Roman rule.

A. Pharisees
B. Essenes
C. Zealots
D. Sadducees

_______ **7.** Why did the Romans persecute Christians during the reign of Nero?

A. Romans were intolerant of any religion.
B. Christians refused to worship the state gods and emperors.
C. Christians started a fire that destroyed much of Rome.
D. Nero converted to Christianity.

_______ **8.** What did the Edict of Milan proclaim?

A. Christianity was the new state religion of the Roman Empire.
B. The Roman Empire was ended.
C. Christians were traitors to the Roman state.
D. Christianity would be officially tolerated.

_______ **9.** Which Roman official ordered the execution of Jesus?

A. Pontius Pilate
B. Constantine
C. Nero
D. Diocletian

NAME________________________ DATE ____________ CLASS ____________

Lesson Quiz 8-2

networks

The Byzantine Empire and Emerging Europe

DIRECTIONS: Completion Enter the appropriate word(s) to complete the statement.

1. A period of civil war followed the death of ____________, the last of the five good emperors, in A.D. 180.

2. The term ____________ means "rule by four."

3. Diocletian tried to set wage and price controls for the empire in order to fight ____________.

4. The city of ____________ was the capital of the Eastern Roman Empire and a "New Rome."

5. Rome was invaded by the ____________ in 410 and by the ____________ in 455.

DIRECTIONS: Multiple Choice Indicate the answer choice that best completes the statement or answers the question.

_______ **6.** What change did Diocletian make to the governmental structure of the Roman Empire?

- **A.** He moved the seat of government to a "New Rome" in the eastern part of the empire.
- **B.** He deposed Romulus Augustulus and made himself emperor.
- **C.** He divided the empire into four units, called prefectures.
- **D.** He changed the state religion to Christianity.

_______ **7.** In the third century, plague outbreaks led to

- **A.** a labor shortage.
- **B.** an invasion by the Sassanid Persians.
- **C.** important medical breakthroughs.
- **D.** new methods of farming.

_______ **8.** Constantine established a "New Rome" at the site of the Greek city of Byzantium because

- **A.** it had a good climate for farming.
- **B.** it already had palaces and a large amphitheater.
- **C.** it was where he was born.
- **D.** it was a strategic location for protecting the eastern frontier of the Roman Empire.

_______ **9.** By the fifth century, the western part of the Roman Empire was controlled mainly by

- **A.** Huns.
- **B.** Sassanid Persians.
- **C.** Germans.
- **D.** the Roman military.

NAME ____________________ DATE ____________ CLASS ____________

Lesson Quiz 8-3

networks

The Byzantine Empire and Emerging Europe

DIRECTIONS: Matching Match each item with the correct statement below.

_____ **1.** pope who extended papal power over the Christian church in the west

_____ **2.** nun who founded the first convent in Germany

_____ **3.** one of four great cities with powerful bishops

_____ **4.** monk who established the basic form of monastic life in the west

_____ **5.** apostle who is considered to be the first pope

A. Benedict

B. Peter

C. Gregory I

D. Leoba

E. Alexandria

DIRECTIONS: Multiple Choice Indicate the answer choice that best completes the statement or answers the question.

_____ **6.** Local Christian communities led by a priest were called

A. bishoprics.
B. parishes.
C. Papal States.
D. monasteries.

_____ **7.** Which of the following is another title for the pope?

A. Bishop of Antioch
B. Bishop of Jerusalem
C. Bishop of Rome
D. Bishop of Alexandria

_____ **8.** Which of the following statements about monasticism is true?

A. Monks were not encouraged to do any physical work because it would distract them from prayer.
B. Monks provided schools for the young and hospitals for the sick.
C. Monks were always solitary hermits who gave up civilization to pursue a spiritual life.
D. Monks lived by a strict rule of behavior that was written by Gregory the Great.

_____ **9.** People sent out to carry a religious message in hopes of converting them are called

A. abbesses.
B. nuns.
C. bishops.
D. missionaries.

NAME ______________________________ DATE ______________ CLASS __________

Lesson Quiz 8-4

networks

The Byzantine Empire and Emerging Europe

DIRECTIONS: Completion Enter the appropriate word(s) to complete the statement.

1. In the kingdoms of the Ostrogoths and Visigoths, Romans were ______________________ power.

2. Clovis established the kingdom of the ______________________.

3. In Germanic law, the fine paid by a wrongdoer to his or her victim's family was called ______________________.

4. The ______________________ was a means of determining guilt in Germanic law.

5. Charlemagne created the ______________________ Empire.

DIRECTIONS: Multiple Choice Indicate the answer choice that best completes the statement or answers the question.

_________ **6.** What happened to the Roman structure of government when the Ostrogoths and the Visigoths took over Roman territories in Italy and Spain?

A. They replaced it with a German style of government.

B. They kept the Roman structure of government, even allowing Roman former officials to keep their jobs.

C. They kept the Roman structure of government but excluded Romans from holding power.

D. They gave all power to the Roman Catholic Church and let it run the government.

_________ **7.** What caused Clovis to convert to Christianity?

A. His wife convinced him to convert.

B. During battle, he made a promise that if he won the battle, he would convert.

C. The pope promised him political support if he converted.

D. Jesus appeared to him in a dream, inspiring him to convert.

_________ **8.** What was the most important social institution in Germanic custom?

A. the state

B. the village

C. the parish

D. the family

NAME_______________________________ DATE _____________ CLASS __________

Lesson Quiz 8-5

networks

The Byzantine Empire and Emerging Europe

DIRECTIONS: Modified True/False In the blank, indicate whether the statement is true (T) or false (F). If false edit the statement to make it a true statement.

_______ **1.** The official language of the Byzantine Empire was Latin.

____

____

_______ **2.** Silk production was an important industry in the Byzantine Empire.

____

____

_______ **3.** The Hippodrome was a large amphitheater where chariot races were held.

____

____

_______ **4.** Leo III outlawed crucifixes as idolatry.

____

DIRECTIONS: Multiple Choice Indicate the answer choice that best completes the statement or answers the question.

_______ **5.** Who was Belisarius?

A. the Byzantine emperor who rebuilt Constantinople in the sixth century

B. the first head of the Eastern Orthodox Church

C. a monk who defended the use of icons

D. the general who led Justinian's army and defeated the Ostrogoths in Italy

_______ **6.** Which of the following statements about *The Body of Civil Law* is true?

A. It was a codification of Roman law, written in Latin.

B. It was a codification of Roman law, written in German.

C. It was a codification of Islamic law, written in Greek.

D. It was a codification of Byzantine law, written in Greek

_______ **7.** The official language of the Eastern Roman Empire was ______________ and the official religion was ______________.

A. Latin/Christianity

B. Greek/Islam

C. Latin/Roman gods and emperors

D. Greek/Christianity

_______ **8.** The ______________ dynasty ruled the Byzantine Empire in the tenth and eleventh centuries.

A. Justinian

B. Seljuk Turk

C. Macedonian

D. Persian

NAME________________________________ DATE ________________ CLASS ____________

Chapter 8 Test, Form A

networks

The Byzantine Empire and Emerging Europe

DIRECTIONS: Matching Match each item with the correct statement below.

________ **1.** infectious disease	**A.** Romulus Augustulus
________ **2.** regular church members	**B.** scriptorium
________ **3.** a type of trial	**C.** laity
________ **4.** capital of the Eastern Roman Empire	**D.** *missi dominici*
________ **5.** harassing to cause suffering	**E.** patriarch
________ **6.** writing room	**F.** Constantinople
________ **7.** deposed emperor of the Western Roman Empire	**G.** pope
________ **8.** head of the Eastern Orthodox Church	**H.** persecution
________ **9.** messengers of the lord king	**I.** ordeal
________ **10.** successor to Peter	**J.** plague

DIRECTIONS: Multiple Choice Indicate the answer choice that best completes the statement or answers the question.

________ **11.** How did monks and nuns help to spread Christianity throughout Europe?

A. by preserving the works of ancient authors
B. by living communally and keeping to a strict schedule of prayer
C. through missionary activities
D. through prayer and manual labor

________ **12.** What did Charlemagne do that merged Roman, Christian, and German elements in his kingdom?

A. He was born a German, converted to Christianity, and learned Latin.
B. As a German king, he modeled his government on the Romans and made Christianity the official religion of the empire.
C. He had the Christian Bible and the works of classical Latin authors translated into German.
D. He, a German king, was crowned emperor of the Romans by the pope.

Chapter 8 Test, Form A *cont.*

networks

The Byzantine Empire and Emerging Europe

_______ **13.** How far had Christianity spread one hundred years after the death of Jesus?

A. Christian churches had been established in most of the major cities of the eastern part of the Roman Empire, mainly attracting members from the Jewish and Greek-speaking populations.

B. Christianity was the official religion of the Roman Empire.

C. Christianity had very few followers and was not known outside of Judaea.

D. Although Christians faced persecution, the Christian community was well established in Rome and had developed a structure based on the leadership of special clergy called bishops.

_______ **14.** Which one of the following statements most accurately reflects the situation in the western half of the Roman Empire in the mid-fifth century?

A. Although it had suffered some invasions by outside forces, it was still relatively intact because of a strong military.

B. After a series of invasions by Visigoths and Vandals, it was becoming a collection of smaller Germanic kingdoms.

C. It was led by a powerful emperor, Romulus Augustulus.

D. It was controlled by the Senate, which was made up of powerful landowners.

_______ **15.** What was the basis for imperial law in the Eastern Roman Empire?

A. Roman law, as codified by Justinian

B. Germanic law, as codified by Charlemagne

C. Islamic law, as codified by the Seljuk Turks

D. Catholic law, as codified by Gregory the Great

_______ **16.** Which emperor made Christianity the official religion of the Roman Empire?

A. Diocletian

B. Constantine

C. Nero

D. Theodosius the Great

_______ **17.** Which of the following statements best describes how Clovis laid the groundwork for the Carolingian Empire?

A. He formed an alliance with the Roman Catholic Church.

B. He was a great patron of the arts.

C. He established the Frankish kingdom and converted to Christianity.

D. He divided his kingdom between his three sons.

_______ **18.** How did Gregory the Great strengthen the papacy?

A. He took control of Rome and surrounding territories, which gave the papacy a source of political power.

B. He established a rule for monasticism that provided a model for monks and nuns throughout Europe.

C. As chief apostle, he received the keys to the kingdom of heaven from Jesus.

D. He built an army to defend the Roman Catholic Church from non-Christian forces.

_______ **19.** Which of the following may have contributed to the decline and fall of the Roman Empire?

A. too much emphasis on agriculture and the arts

B. lack of a strong authoritarian government

C. population decline due to plague and lack of a workable political system

D. a weak military

_______ **20.** What issues did the Byzantine Empire face in the eleventh century?

A. plague and invasions by Ostrogoths and Visigoths

B. schism with the Roman Catholic Church in the west and the advance of the Seljuk Turks

C. schism with Islam and a declining silk industry

D. plague and riots following chariot races

The Byzantine Empire and Emerging Europe

DIRECTIONS: Essay Answer the following questions on a separate piece of paper.

21. Describe the organization and leadership of the Christian Church that emerged in the fourth century.

22. Explain the policies of Diocletian and Constantine. How were their policies alike? How were they different?

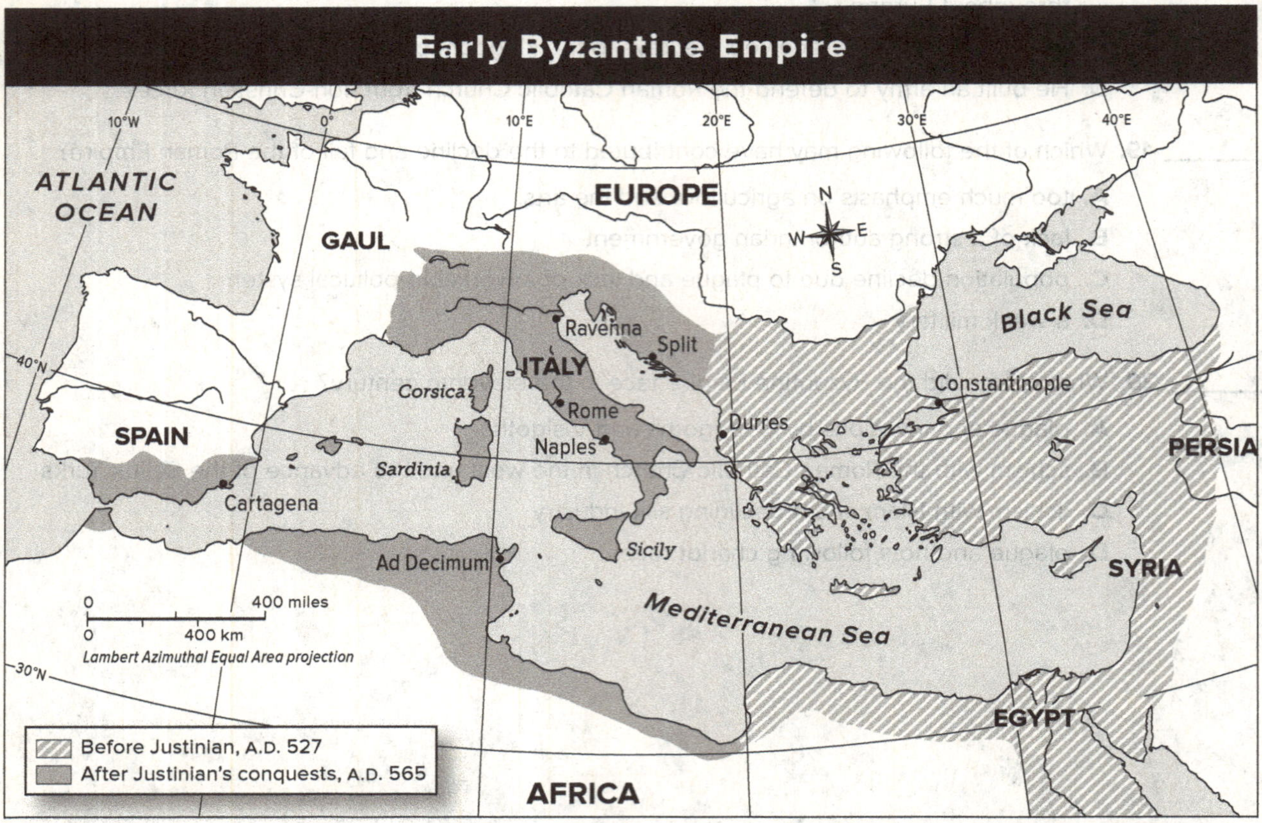

23. Using the map and information in the chapter, describe Justinian's accomplishments.

Chapter 8 Test, Form B

networks

The Byzantine Empire and Emerging Europe

DIRECTIONS: Short Answer Answer each of the following questions on a separate piece of paper.

"[Clovis said] 'Jesus Christ, who, as Clotilda declares, are the son of the living God . . . who are worthy to give aid to those in distress and to give victory to those who have faith in you, devoutly I beg your glorious aid, so that . . . I shall believe and be baptized in your name. For I have called upon my own gods but, as I find, they are far from helping me; hence I believe that they are endowed with no power whatever, since they give no aid to those who obey them. I now invoke you, I long to believe in you, so that I may even be overwhelmed by my enemies.' When he said this, the Alamanni turned and began to retreat in flight."

—Gregory of Tours, from *The History of the Franks*, sixth century

1. Based on the quotation above, what made Clovis leave his faith and convert to Christianity?

2. Based on the quotation above, what does Clovis know about Jesus from Clotilda?

"[You] have clothed yourselves with the new self, which is being renewed in knowledge according to the image of its creator. In that renewal there is no longer Greek and Jew, . . . barbarian, Scythian, slave and free; but Christ is all and in all! As God's chosen ones, holy and beloved, clothe yourselves with compassion, kindness, humility, meekness, patience. Bear with one another and, if anyone has a complaint against one another, forgive each other; just as the Lord has forgiven you, so you also must forgive. Above all, clothe yourselves with love, which binds everything together in perfect harmony."

—Colossians 3: 10–14

3. Based on the passage above, why do you think Christianity appealed to all classes, but especially to the poor and powerless?

4. Based on the passage above, why do you think Roman officials might have found Christianity threatening?

Chapter 8 Test, Form B *cont.*

networks

The Byzantine Empire and Emerging Europe

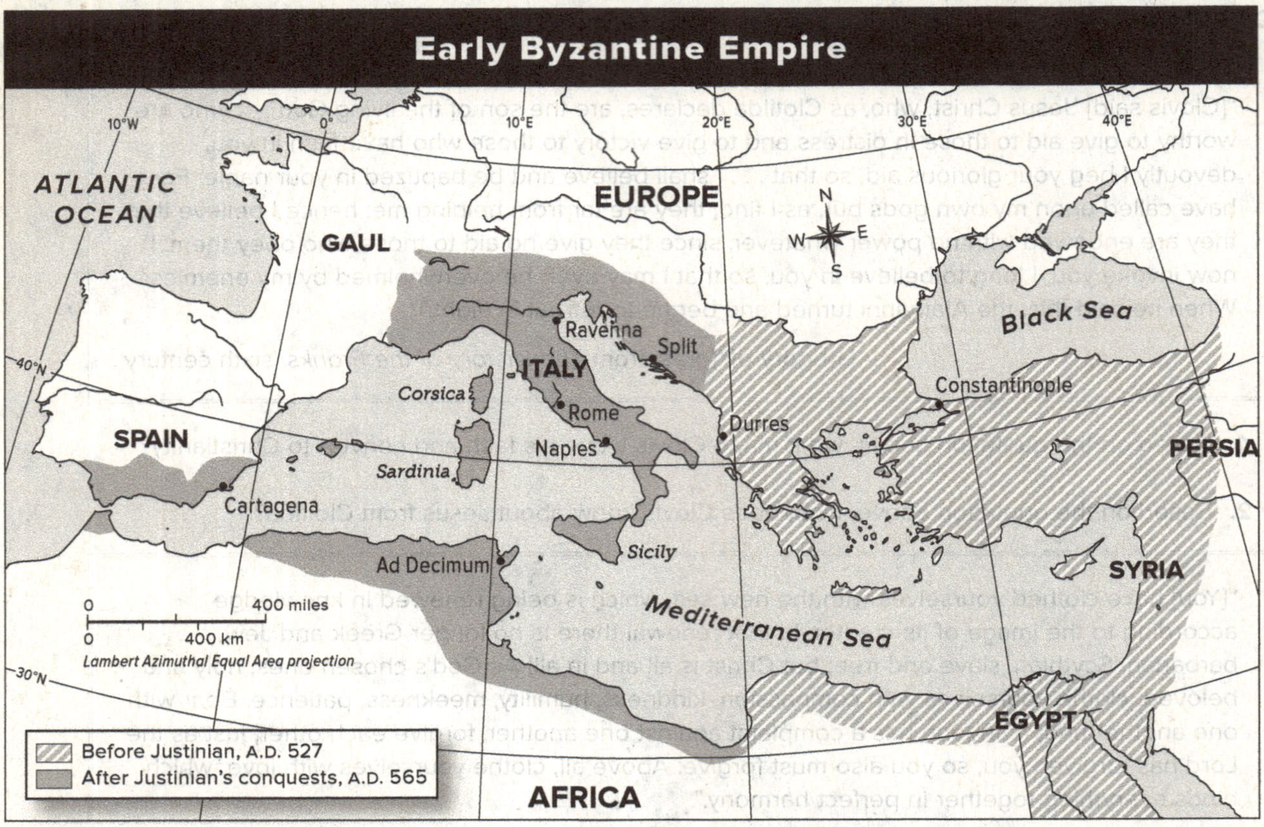

5. Based on the map above, how far west did Justinian's empire stretch?

6. Based on the map above, how far east did his empire stretch?

DIRECTIONS: Essay Answer the following question on a separate piece of paper.

7. Christianity began with a single man, Jesus, and his followers and grew to transform not only the Roman Empire, but also the empires that followed it. Use the content taught in this chapter to explain the chapter's Enduring Understanding statement: *New ideas and beliefs, along with influence from individual leaders, can transform empires and change the shape of history.*

NAME ______________________________ DATE ______________ CLASS ______________

Lesson Quiz 9-1

networks

Islam and the Arab Empire

DIRECTIONS: Matching Match each item with the correct statement below.

________ **1.** the acts of worship practiced by Muslims		**A.** Allah
________ **2.** the code of law that regulates all aspects of Muslim life		**B.** Five Pillars of Islam
________ **3.** a divine truth revealed to Muhammad		**C.** *Hijrah*
________ **4.** the journey of Muhammad and his followers to Medina		**D.** revelation
________ **5.** the god of Islam		**E.** *shari'ah*

DIRECTIONS: Multiple Choice Indicate the answer choice that best completes the statement or answers the question.

________ **6.** Before the trade routes were established, Arabs were primarily

A. enslaved people. **C.** nomads.
B. hunter-gatherers. **D.** warriors.

________ **7.** What led directly to Arabs populating more of the desert in the first millennium B.C.?

A. attacks by invading armies of Persians
B. the domestication of the camel
C. the flooding of the Nile river
D. war with Greece

________ **8.** The Islamic religion was created as a direct result of

A. the revelations received by Muhammad.
B. the teachings of Jesus.
C. the Ten Commandments received by Moses.
D. the trade practices of Arab merchants.

________ **9.** For early Arabs, Allah was symbolized by

A. a figure of a fish. **C.** a sacred stone.
B. a figure of the moon. **D.** a star.

________ **10.** According to Islamic teaching, Muhammad received messages from

A. Gabriel.
B. Jesus.
C. Khadija.
D. Moses.

NAME_______________________________________ DATE ________________ CLASS ____________

Lesson Quiz 9-2

networks

Islam and the Arab Empire

DIRECTIONS: Completion Enter the appropriate word(s) to complete the statement.

1. Since Muhammad had named no successor before he died, his followers chose Abū Bakr, Muhammed's adviser and ______________________, to be their religious and political leader.

2. Early caliphs ruled their empire from the city of ______________________.

3. When General Mu'āwiyah made the position of caliph hereditary, he established the ______________________ dynasty.

4. The ______________________ were a pastoral people in North Africa who were conquered and converted to Islam by the Arabs.

5. Arab expansion in Western Europe was halted when Arab armies were defeated at the Battle of ______________________.

DIRECTIONS: Multiple Choice Indicate the answer choice that best completes the statement or answers the question.

_________ 6. Abū Bakr unified the Muslim world by

- **A.** distributing the wealth of rich merchants to poor people throughout the Muslim world.
- **B.** encouraging tribes to solve their disputes through discussion and compromise.
- **C.** granting freedom of religion throughout the Arab Empire.
- **D.** suppressing political and religious uprisings.

_________ 7. When Abū Bakr died,

- **A.** a committee of tribal leaders was formed to rule the Arab Empire.
- **B.** conflicts over who should rule resulted in several assassinations.
- **C.** his son took over the leadership of the Arab Empire.
- **D.** Muslim leadership of the Arab Empire was challenged by Christian opponents.

_________ 8. In 636, the Arab army took advantage of a dust storm army to defeat

- **A.** the army of the Russian Empire.
- **B.** the Byzantine army.
- **C.** a group of dissenting tribes within the Arab Empire.
- **D.** the Spanish army.

_________ 9. In 680, what event led Islam to split into two conflicting groups?

- **A.** the entry of new ethnic groups into the Arab Empire
- **B.** the defeat of Arab forces in Gaul
- **C.** a revolt in Iraq led by the son of Muhammad's son-in-law
- **D.** the unsuccessful attack by Muslim forces on Constantinople

NAME_______________ DATE _______________ CLASS _______________

Lesson Quiz 9-3

networks

Islam and the Arab Empire

DIRECTIONS: Modified True/False In the blank, indicate whether the statement is true (T) or false (F). If false edit the statement to make it a true statement.

_______ **1.** As a result of trade, the Arab Empire was less urbanized than most of the rest of the world.

____

____

_______ **2.** The belief that all Muslims were equal in the eyes of Allah led to a classless society in the Arab world.

____

____

_______ **3.** Slavery was widespread in the Islamic world.

____

____

_______ **4.** The mathematical discipline of geometry was first developed by an Arab mathematician.

____

____

DIRECTIONS: Multiple Choice Indicate the answer choice that best completes the statement or answers the question.

_______ **5.** Arab trade routes extended

A. from Baghdad to Constantinople.
B. from Damascus to Cairo.
C. from east of Makkah to Madinah.
D. from Morocco to beyond the Caspian Sea.

_______ **6.** Devout Muslims are prohibited from

A. drinking wine.
B. getting married.
C. making pilgrimages.
D. reading the Quran aloud.

_______ **7.** The custom of requiring women to cover virtually all parts of their bodies in public

A. is not practiced anywhere today.
B. was an Arab practice.
C. was common only outside of cities.
D. was required by the Quran.

Chapter 9 Test, Form A

networks

Islam and the Arab Empire

DIRECTIONS: Matching Match each item with the correct statement below.

_______ **1.** early converts to Islam who lived in the desert

_______ **2.** pre-Islamic belief in multiple gods

_______ **3.** holy scriptures of Islam

_______ **4.** group that accepts only Umayyads as the true rulers of Islam

_______ **5.** group that accepts only the descendants of Ali as the true rulers of Islam

_______ **6.** journey of Muhammad and his followers to Madinah

_______ **7.** "struggle in the way of god"

_______ **8.** secular and spiritual leader of an Islamic community

_______ **9.** the distinctive tower of a mosque

_______ **10.** scientist who wrote a medical encyclopedia stressing the contagious nature of disease

A. bedouins

B. caliph

C. *Hijrah*

D. Ibn Sīnā

E. jihad

F. minaret

G. polytheism

H. Quran

I. Shia

J. Sunni

DIRECTIONS: Multiple Choice Indicate the answer choice that best completes the statement or answers the question.

_______ **11.** Muhammad began to meditate in the hills because

A. he was troubled by the gap between the generosity of most people and the greed of the wealthy elite.

B. he was trying to think of a solution to a problem that his wife had.

C. the hills were a holy site that was supposed to give visions to worthy individuals.

D. sinners overran the town of Makkah.

_______ **12.** After Muhammad's death, Muslim scholars drew up the shari'ah, which is

A. a collection of Muhammad's sayings that were not included in the Quran.

B. an elaborate burial ritual still performed at Muslim funerals today.

C. a code that provides believers with practical laws to regulate their daily lives.

D. a map to a holy shrine in Makkah.

Chapter 9 Test, Form A *cont.*

networks

Islam and the Arab Empire

_______ **13.** One of Five Pillars of Islam, the hajj, is

A. the observation of the holy month of July, including fasting from dawn to sunset.

B. one's duty to give alms to the poor and unfortunate.

C. a pilgrimage to Makkah.

D. a public prayer at midday on Friday to worship Allah.

_______ **14.** As the Arab Empire grew, people who were not Muslims or did not convert to Islam in the conquered territories

A. had to give up all of their property to the empire.

B. had to pay special taxes.

C. were banished from those territories.

D. were imprisoned for at least five years.

_______ **15.** By the time the Umayyad dynasty was established, the Arab Empire had already conquered

A. the Austro-Hungarian Empire.

B. the Persian Empire.

C. southern France and Corsica.

D. Switzerland.

_______ **16.** The revolt led by Hussein during the early Umayyad period led to

A. a bloody war that lasted just seven days.

B. the destruction of the burial place of Muhammad.

C. the split of Islam into two separate groups.

D. the strengthening of the Umayyad dynasty.

_______ **17.** The Umayyad dynasty was replaced by

A. Abbasid rulers.

B. Bedouin rulers.

C. Egyptian rulers.

D. Sunni rulers.

_______ **18.** Through the achievements of Muslim scholars, Europeans

A. developed an appreciation for painting and sculpture.

B. discovered tobacco.

C. were able to obtain products from Spain.

D. were able to read the works of Aristotle and other Greek philosophers.

______ **19.** A crucial part of every Muslim city or town was the ________, which was a covered market.

A. bazaar

B. caliphate

C. mosque

D. sheikh

______ **20.** During the Abbasid dynasty, the council that advised the caliph was led by a prime minister known as

A. an arabesque.

B. an astrolabe.

C. a sultan.

D. a vizier.

DIRECTIONS: Essay Answer the following questions on a separate sheet of paper.

21. Explain in detail how the scientific advances of the Arab Empire made an impact on the Western world.

"Perhaps . . . another kind of explanation can be given for the acceptance of Arab rule by the population of the conquered countries. To most of them it did not much matter whether they were ruled by Iranians, Greeks or Arabs. Government impinged for the most part on the life of cities. . . .

"[C]ity-dwellers might not care much who ruled them, provided they were secure, at peace and reasonably taxed. The people of the countryside . . . lived under their own chiefs and . . . with their own customs, and it made little difference to them who ruled the cities. For some, the replacement of Greeks and Iranians by Arabs even offered advantages."

—Albert Hourani, *A History of the Arab Peoples,* 1991

22. Read the passage above. Based on what you know of the Arab Empire, explain how life might have stayed the same or changed for city dwellers in countries that were conquered by the Arab Empire.

Chapter 9 Test, Form B

networks

Islam and the Arab Empire

DIRECTIONS: Short Answer Answer each of the following questions on a separate sheet of paper.

Five Pillars of Islam

Belief (Shahaadatayn)	Prayer (Salaah)	Charity (Zakaah)	Fasting (Siyaam)	Pilgrimage (Hajj)
Believing there is no deity but the One God, and Muhammad is his messenger	Performing the prescribed prayers five times a day	Giving part of one's wealth to the poor ("giving alms")	Refraining from food and drink from dawn to sunset through the month of Ramadan	Making a pilgrimage to Makkah once in a lifetime
Quran				

1. Based on this chart, explain how Charity (*Zakaah*) is different from the other Pillars of Islam.

2. According to the chart, which of the Five Pillars of Islam require individuals to perform physical tasks, and which do not?

> "By the time I was ten I had mastered the [Quran] and a great deal of literature, so I was marveled at for my aptitude. . . . I now occupied myself with mastering the various texts and commentaries on natural science and metaphysics, until all the gates of knowledge were open to me. Next I desired to study medicine, and . . . [proceeded] to read all the books that have been written on this subject. Medicine is not a difficult science, and naturally I excelled in it in a very short time, so that qualified physicians began to read medicine with me.
> The next eighteen months I devoted entirely to reading; I studied Logic once again, and all the parts of philosophy."
>
> —Ibn Sina, eleventh century

3. According to this passage, what subjects did the author choose to study first?

4. Why does the author use the term "master" instead of "study" when he refers to the subjects he was learning?

Chapter 9 Test, Form B *cont.*

networks

Islam and the Arab Empire

> "Ramazan [Ramadan] . . . is an occasion during which believers are thought to be closer to God. Ramazan is a month-long period of fasting, somewhat like Lent only more stringent. It is a time of atonement. It is the month in which the Qur'an was allegedly revealed to Muhammed. It is said: 'When the noble time of Ramazan comes, the doors of heaven are opened, the doors of hell closed, and the devils tied down.' In other words, people's souls are opened to God and closed to *seytan* (devils); they are sustained by God as by food."
>
> —Carol Delaney, *The Seed and the Soil: Gender and Cosmology in Turkish Village Society,* 1991

5. According to the passage, what does Ramadan mark?

6. How does Ramadan fit into the Five Pillars of Islam?

DIRECTIONS: Essay Answer the following question on a separate piece of paper.

7. The religion of Islam had an enormous effect on all aspects of the lives of people in the Arab Empire and on the structure of the empire itself. Think about the effects that Islam has had on the nations and peoples of the Arab Empire. Then use the content taught in this chapter to explain the chapter's Enduring Understanding Statement: *Religion can bring about significant cultural changes, becoming the basis for new political and social systems within empires.*

NAME ____________________ DATE ____________ CLASS ____________

Lesson Quiz 10-1

networks

Medieval Kingdoms in Europe

DIRECTIONS: Matching Match each item with the correct statement below.

______ **1.** armed cavalry		**A.** fief
______ **2.** Germanic warriors from Scandinavia		**B.** knights
______ **3.** grant of land to a vassal		**C.** chivalry
______ **4.** code of ethics guiding nobility		**D.** feudalism
______ **5.** relationship between lords and vassals		**E.** Vikings

DIRECTIONS: Multiple Choice Indicate the answer choice that best completes the statement or answers the question.

______ **6.** Which of these would directly serve both lords and kings?

A. knights

B. peasants

C. serfs

D. vassals

______ **7.** The lord-vassal relationship

A. implied a sense of servitude.

B. was between knights who served the king.

C. required military service.

D. was governed by strict authoritarian rules.

______ **8.** Which of the following names two problems facing western Europe after the death of Charlemagne?

A. invasions from northern peoples and internal division

B. disagreements over the roles of women and issues with succession

C. invasions from southern peoples and food shortages

D. religious divisions and the need to document the laws of feudalism

______ **9.** Why was feudalism developed?

A. There was a need for a clear successor to the crown.

B. Centralized power was lost in the face of invasion.

C. The church was losing power and failed to protect the lords.

D. Lords decided to reform society by establishing chivalry.

______ **10.** Which of following was an expectation of knights under the chivalric code?

A. to settle disputes with invaders

B. to treat prisoners with respect and dignity

C. to fight one another to the death in tournaments

D. to give women a voice in government

NAME_______________________ DATE ____________ CLASS ____________

Lesson Quiz 10-2

networks

Medieval Kingdoms in Europe

DIRECTIONS: Matching Match each item with the correct statement below.

_______ **1.** a heavy, wheeled plow with an iron plowshare

_______ **2.** wealthy, powerful landowner

_______ **3.** agricultural estate that a lord ran and peasants worked

_______ **4.** peasant legally bound to the land who had to provide labor services, pay rents, and be subject to the lord's control

_______ **5.** the middle class, including merchants, industrialists, and professional people

A. patrician

B. serfs

C. *carruca*

D. manor

E. bourgeoisie

DIRECTIONS: Multiple Choice Indicate the answer choice that best completes the statement or answers the question.

_______ **6.** In order to encourage trade between Flanders and Italy, the counts of Champagne

A. built a canal between the two, upon which their town was a major stopping point.

B. offered free wine to traders traveling through their fiefdom.

C. initiated a series of trade fairs in the chief towns of the territory.

D. agreed not to marry the merchants of these two countries.

_______ **7.** The Hanseatic League was instrumental in

A. forming a union between Belgium and France.

B. protecting trade and promoting the economy in Northern Europe.

C. encouraging the making of silk and woolen cloth for sale in the East.

D. devising the system of capitalism, which involved investing in trade for profit.

_______ **8.** Which of these may have enabled people to move back into cities?

A. less dependence on agriculture for survival

B. less control of feudal lords over peasants

C. dangerous invasions of outside groups

D. expansion of legal rights for artisans

_______ **9.** Which of these was a result of the growth of trade and cities in the Middle Ages?

A. the decline of the middle class

B. increased dependence on the land and relationship to a lord

C. people acquiring rights and freedoms from local lords

D. improved sanitation and living conditions

Lesson Quiz 10-3

networks

Medieval Kingdoms in Europe

DIRECTIONS: Matching Match each item with the correct statement below.

_______ **1.** protected the Pope and assumed the title that had belonged to Charlemagne

_______ **2.** Great Charter that codified rights of kings and vassals

_______ **3.** a uniform system of law that developed in England

_______ **4.** a social or political class

_______ **5.** settled in Kiev and began trade with Byzantines

A. Magna Carta

B. common law

C. Oleg

D. estate

E. Otto I

DIRECTIONS: Multiple Choice Indicate the answer choice that best completes the statement or answers the question.

_______ **6.** The representative government that emerged in thirteenth-century England was called _______________.

A. Parliament.

B. the Domesday Book.

C. the royal courts.

D. the Roman Catholic Church.

_______ **7.** The Battle of Hastings determined the language and ruling class of _______________ in the High Middle Ages.

A. Kievan Rus

B. the Mongols

C. France

D. England

_______ **8.** French territories, including _______________ and Maine, were reclaimed from the English by _______________.

A. Hastings; Philip II Augustus

B. Aquitaine; Frederick I

C. Normandy; Philip II Augustus

D. Anjou; Frederick I

_______ **9.** Eastern Slavs converted to _______________, and _______________ helped them become literate.

A. Orthodox Christianity; Vladimir

B. Roman Catholicism; Thomas à Becket

C. Orthodox Christianity; Cyril

D. Roman Catholicism; King John

Chapter 10 Test, Form A

networks

Medieval Kingdoms in Europe

DIRECTIONS: Matching Match each item with the correct statement below.

_______ **1.** contest where knights could show their fighting skills		**A.** Domesday Book
_______ **2.** Hungarians		**B.** fief
_______ **3.** the grant of land made to a vassal		**C.** Philip IV
_______ **4.** first census in Europe since Roman times		**D.** Magyars
_______ **5.** created the first French parliament		**E.** Mongols
_______ **6.** won the Battle of Hastings		**F.** tournament
_______ **7.** gave written recognition to the mutual rights and obligations between kings and vassals		**G.** William of Normandy
		H. Kievan Rus
_______ **8.** converted the Eastern Slavs to Orthodox Christianity		**I.** Magna Carta
_______ **9.** conquered Russia in the thirteenth century		**J.** Cyril
_______ **10.** settled by Oleg the Viking in the tenth century		

DIRECTIONS: Multiple Choice Indicate the answer choice that best completes the statement or answers the question.

_______ **11.** In return for protecting the pope, Otto I was

A. granted land in Normandy.
B. crowned Roman emperor.
C. linked to Byzantium.
D. converted to Christianity.

_______ **12.** Eastern Slavic people were converted to Christianity by

A. Byzantine missionaries.
B. Viking nuns.
C. Frankish monks.
D. Roman priests.

Chapter 10 Test, Form A *cont.*

Medieval Kingdoms in Europe

_______ **13.** Native peoples in Russia and Ukraine were conquered by

A. Vikings, then Mongols.

B. Slavs, then Christians.

C. Mongols, then Vikings.

D. Franks, then Moors.

_______ **14.** Orthodox Christianity became the chief religion for the

A. Polish.

B. Bohemians.

C. Britons.

D. Serbs.

_______ **15.** The Vikings were made part of European civilization by

A. their widespread invasions of Asian kingdoms.

B. the conquest of Scandinavia in 911 by Charlemagne.

C. the Frankish policy of settling them and converting them to Christianity.

D. their desire to sail to America.

_______ **16.** The most important gift a lord could give to a vassal was

A. a piece of land.

B. a dragon boat.

C. his daughter in marriage.

D. a gold ring.

_______ **17.** Which of the following was a code of ethics knights were to uphold?

A. Chivalry

B. The fief

C. The Magna Carta

D. The Domesday Book

_______ **18.** At the heart of feudalism was

A. the knight, who was the enforcer of the lord and a protector of the lord's lands.

B. serfdom, which meant that all non-vassals labored to support the serfs.

C. the grant of serfs made to loyal vassals, which was known as a fief.

D. vassalage, which meant warriors swore loyalty to a lord, who in turn took care of their needs.

_______ **19.** Philip II Augustus greatly increased the power of the French monarchy by

A. forming the first French parliament by meeting with representatives of the three estates.

B. expanding the royal mint.

C. waging war on the rulers of England and gaining control of Normandy, Maine, Anjou, and Aquitaine.

D. defeating King William at the Battle of Hastings.

_______ **20.** How did craft guilds improve economic conditions in cities?

A. encouraged competition among workers

B. set quality standards for goods produced

C. organized workers to strike

D. kept women out of the workforce

DIRECTIONS: Short Answer Answer each of the following questions.

> "In the year of the Lord's Incarnation [885], (the thirty-seventh of King Alfred's life), the Viking army split up into two bands: one band set out for [the East Frankish kingdom], and the other, coming to Britain, entered Kent and besieged the city which in English is called Rochester, situated on the eastern bank of the river Medway. The Vikings immediately constructed a strong fortification for themselves in front of its entrance, but they were unable to capture the city because the citizens defended themselves courageously until King Alfred arrived, bringing them relief with a large army. Thereupon the Vikings, abandoning their fortress, . . . fled quickly to their ships."
>
> —from Asser's *Life of King Alfred*, 884

21. The passage above describes a scene that was common in ninth-century Europe. Explain how this led to a new social and political order. Describe the new order, including the relationships of people involved.

____

____

____

____

____

Chapter 10 Test, Form A *cont.*

networks

Medieval Kingdoms in Europe

22. Improvements in agriculture during the Middle Ages led to a population increase. Describe these improvements and explain why they were important.

NAME________________________ DATE ______________ CLASS __________

Chapter 10 Test, Form B

networks

Medieval Kingdoms in Europe

DIRECTIONS: Short Answer Answer each of the following questions on a separate piece of paper.

> "The man should put his hands together as a sign of humility, and place them between the two hands of his lord as a token that he vows everything to him and promises faith to him; and the lord should receive him and promise to keep faith with him. Then the man should say: 'Sir, I enter your homage and faith and become your man by mouth and hands, and I swear and promise to keep faith and loyalty to you against all others."
>
> —from *A Source Book for Medieval History*

1. What medieval socio-political system is described in this passage? Cite evidence from the passage to support your answer.

2. Why did this system come into being, and what purpose did it serve?

3. What part did a fief play in this new system?

Europe, 1160

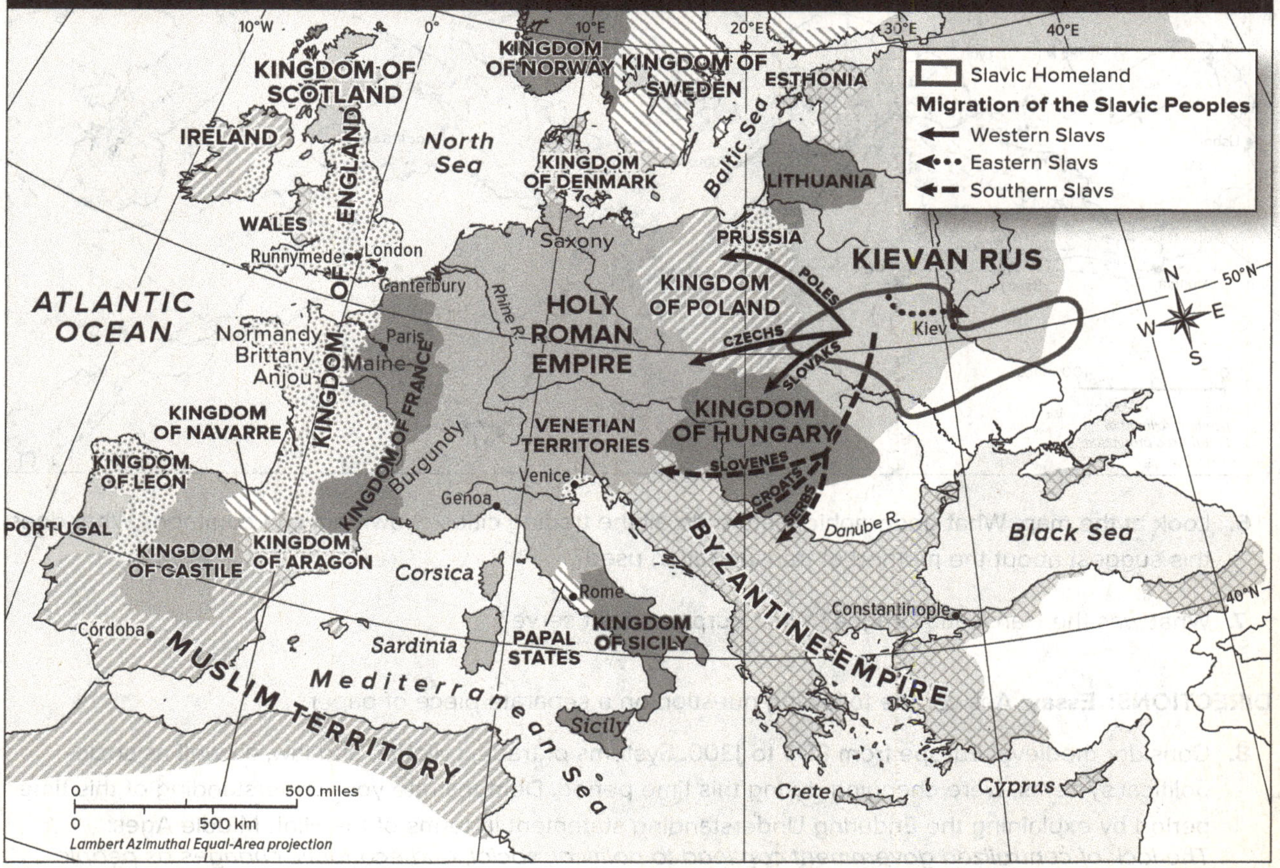

4. Look at the map on the previous page. Recall and state the religions that both Western and Eastern Slavic people converted to. How might geography have influenced religious conversion?

5. Vikings invaded the lands of the Slavic people, founding Kiev. Eventually the city became a powerful trade center in the eleventh century. Use the map on the previous page to determine why this might have been the case.

Medieval Centers of Trade, after 1100

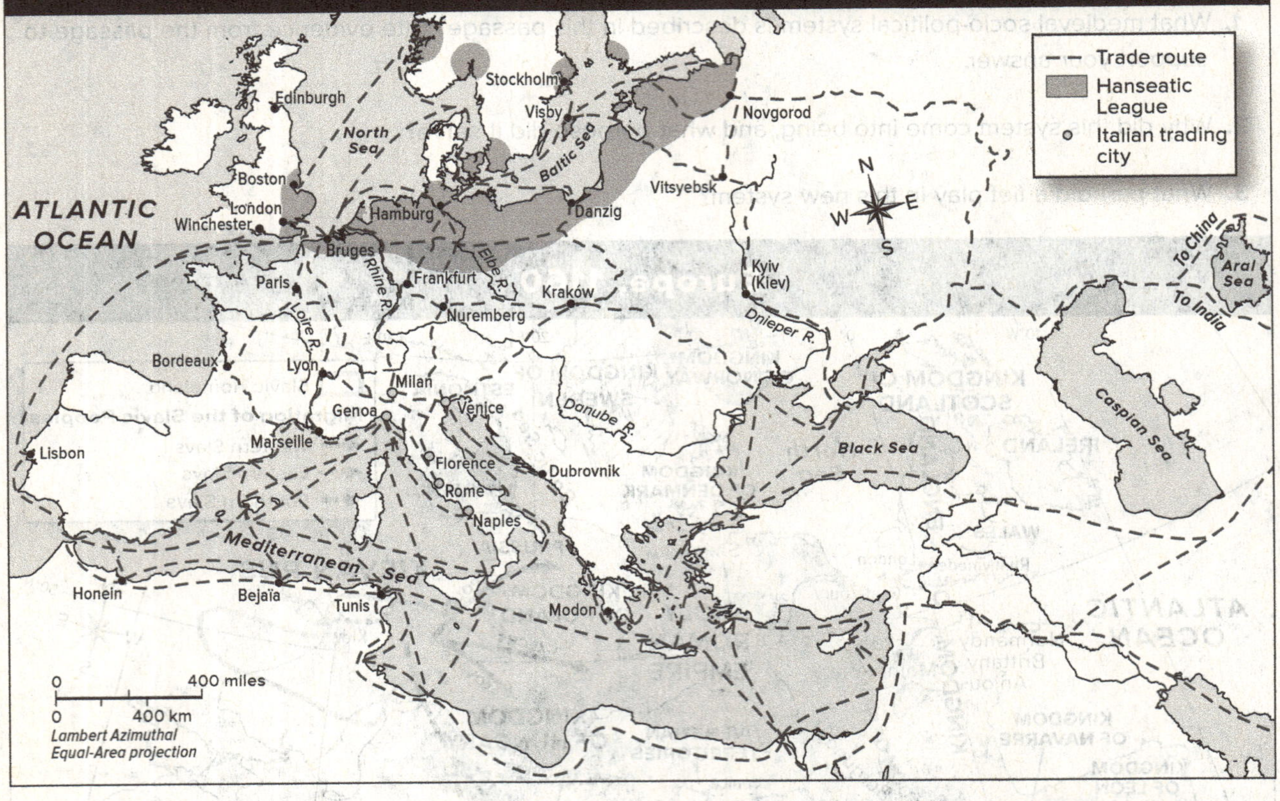

6. Look at the map. What geographic feature do all the trading cities shown have in common? What does this suggest about the method of transportation used?

7. What was the Hanseatic League? What purpose did it serve?

DIRECTIONS: Essay Answer the following question on a separate piece of paper.

8. Consider medieval Europe from 800 to 1300. Systems of trade, religion, and law, as well as socio-political systems, were changing during this time period. Demonstrate your understanding of this time period by explaining the Enduring Understanding statement in terms of the High Middle Ages: *The lack of centralized government can lead to political, social, and economic changes as people seek other sources of stability and protection.*

NAME____________________ DATE ____________ CLASS ________

Lesson Quiz 11-1

networks

Civilizations of East Asia

DIRECTIONS: Matching Match each item with the correct statement below.

_______ **1.** dynasty that reunified China from 581 to 618

_______ **2.** reform rulers from this dynasty restored Chinese power in East Asia

_______ **3.** principles underlying Chinese government

_______ **4.** a time of cultural achievement in China from 960 to 1279

_______ **5.** an important factor in increased foreign trade

A. Sui dynasty

B. Silk Road

C. Song dynasty

D. Tang dynasty

E. Confucian ideals

DIRECTIONS: Multiple Choice Indicate the answer choice that best completes the statement or answers the question.

_______ **6.** Which term best describes the time period between the Han and Sui dynasties?

A. corruption
B. the Song dynasty
C. the Tang dynasty
D. disorder

_______ **7.** One accomplishment of the Tang dynasty was

A. the creation of a civil service exam.
B. the avoidance of corruption in government.
C. the establishment of diplomatic relations with states in Southeast Asia.
D. the offering of tribute to Korea.

_______ **8.** By the time of the Song,

A. private merchants were active and guilds had begun to appear.
B. the practice of giving a dowry had ended.
C. the scholar-gentry had diminished in importance.
D. China had closed down its trade with other regions.

_______ **9.** Technical knowledge from China that traveled to other regions included techniques for

A. sharecropping.
B. printing.
C. mining precious stones.
D. growing tropical fruits.

NAME________________________ DATE ____________ CLASS ________

Lesson Quiz 11-2

networks

Civilizations of East Asia

DIRECTIONS: Modified True/False In the blank, indicate whether the statement is true (T) or false (F). If false edit the statement to make it a true statement.

________ **1.** The leader who completed the conquest of the Song dynasty was Genghis Khan.

____

____

________ **2.** The Mongols increased their empire and their trade along the main routes to Java, Sumatra, and Japan.

____

____

________ **3.** Cultural advances in China reached their height beginning with the Sui dynasty.

____

____

DIRECTIONS: Multiple Choice Indicate the answer choice that best completes the statement or answers the question.

________ **4.** Who led the Yuan dynasty?

A. Temüjin

B. Genghis Khan

C. Kublai Khan

D. Zhu Yuanzhang

________ **5.** Which dynasty is viewed as the great age of Chinese poetry?

A. Sui dynasty

B. Tang dynasty

C. Song dynasty

D. Yuan dynasty

________ **6.** During which dynasty was printing invented?

A. Sui dynasty

B. Tang dynasty

C. Song dynasty

D. Yuan dynasty

________ **7.** One reason for prosperity and trade during the Mongol Empire was

A. the effect of Buddhist ideals on Mongol culture.

B. the effect of Confucian ideals on Mongol culture.

C. their control of an enormous landmass under a single rule.

D. their support of the arts, especially poetry, which promoted their rule.

NAME ________________________________ DATE ________________ CLASS ____________

Lesson Quiz 11-3

networks

Civilizations of East Asia

DIRECTIONS: Completion Enter the appropriate word(s) to complete the statement.

1. In order to unify Japan, Shōtoku Taishi brought the Chinese form of ________________ to the islands.

2. The power struggles between Japan's central government and aristocrats eventually resulted in the collapse of ________________.

3. Minamoto Yoritomo protected his own interests by means of a military general called a ________________.

4. In literature, women were the most productive writers of ________________.

5. The three kingdoms of early Korea were the ________________, Paekche, and Silla.

DIRECTIONS: Multiple Choice Indicate the answer choice that best completes the statement or answers the question.

______ **6.** Who supported the Silla in gaining control of the entire Korean peninsula?

A. the Koryo dynasty
B. the Tang dynasty
C. the Kamakura shogunate
D. the Paekche kingdom

______ **7.** When Korea was divided into three kingdoms, each was ruled by

A. Buddhist monks.
B. Confucian ideals.
C. Silla kings.
D. a hereditary monarch.

______ **8.** The shogunate was established in Japan in order to

A. strengthen the state.
B. promote internal trade.
C. promote external trade.
D. strengthen the power of the aristocracy.

______ **9.** What was the purpose of the samurai?

A. to end civil wars
B. to collect tax revenues
C. to protect their employers
D. to follow the warrior code of Bushido

______ **10.** The religion that is linked to a belief in the divinity of the emperor and the sacredness of the Japanese nation is

A. Shinto.
B. Buddhism.
C. Daoism.
D. Confucianism.

NAME ______________________ DATE ______________ CLASS __________

Lesson Quiz 11-4

networks

Civilizations of East Asia

DIRECTIONS: Modified True/False In the blank, indicate whether the statement is true (T) or false (F). If false edit the statement to make it a true statement.

________ **1.** As a chain of islands, the Malay world developed a distinct culture.

____

____

________ **2.** Dai Viet, the new Vietnamese state, adopted Christianity.

____

____

________ **3.** For hundreds of years, Buddhism was widely accepted in India.

____

____

________ **4.** A phase of Islamic expansion in South Asia stopped near the end of the tenth century.

____

____

DIRECTIONS: Multiple Choice Indicate the answer choice that best completes the statement or answers the question.

________ **5.** During the 1300s, Mesopotamia and northern India were attacked by

A. the sultanate of Delhi.

B. Timur Lenk from Samarqand.

C. the Japanese.

D. Hindu merchants.

________ **6.** Islam expanded in India with invasions from

A. Korea.

B. Ghazna.

C. China.

D. Japan.

________ **7.** Buddhism in India declined as a result of

A. Confucianism.

B. Christianity.

C. Islam and Shinto.

D. Hinduism and Islam.

________ **8.** Timur Lenk's main effect on India was

A. the decline of the sultanate of Delhi.

B. the decline of Hinduism.

C. the destruction of the Mongol Empire.

D. the emergence of the Mogul Empire.

NAME________________________________ DATE ______________ CLASS ___________

Chapter 11 Test, Form A

networks

Civilizations of East Asia

DIRECTIONS: Matching Match each item with the correct statement below.

_______ **1.** strong ruler who unified the Mongols

_______ **2.** Hindu warriors who fought against Ghazna

_______ **3.** the money, goods, or property that parents were expected to provide a husband's family when their daughter married

_______ **4.** a chain of islands

_______ **5.** emperor who completed the Grand Canal

_______ **6.** "the teachings of the elders"; a school of Buddhism

_______ **7.** dynasty after the Silla

_______ **8.** a strict warrior code by which the samurai lived

_______ **9.** territories created from Genghis Khan's empire

_______ **10.** area north of the Himalaya

A. Bushido

B. dowry

C. Tibet

D. Koryo

E. Theravada

F. Genghis Khan

G. khanates

H. Rajput

I. archipelago

J. Sui Yangdi

DIRECTIONS: Multiple Choice Indicate the answer choice that best completes the statement or answers the question.

_______ **11.** Which of the following is the product of mixing cast iron and wrought iron?

A. gunpowder
B. Song
C. steel
D. fire-lance

_______ **12.** The Song dynasty was overthrown by

A. the Mongols.
B. the Uighurs.
C. the Koreans.
D. Changan.

_______ **13.** The Mongols may have been prevented from conquering western Europe by

A. the Himalaya.

B. the Gupta Empire.

C. Genghis Khan's death.

D. Marco Polo.

_______ **14.** The first Mongol dynasty in China was the

A. Yuan.

B. Khanate.

C. Sui.

D. Champa.

_______ **15.** The Chinese defended themselves against the Mongols with

A. canals.

B. porcelain.

C. siege warfare.

D. gunpowder.

_______ **16.** Prince Shōtoku wanted rulers to be portrayed as

A. democratic.

B. Confucian.

C. writers.

D. divine.

_______ **17.** Zen Buddhism teaches that one way to achieve nirvana is through

A. proper nutrition and eating the correct foods.

B. instantaneous enlightenment or a long process of meditation.

C. strict observance of the warrior's code.

D. evaluating past deeds.

_______ **18.** The school of Buddhism that defines nirvana as not just a release from the "wheel of life" but a true heaven is

A. Mahayana.

B. Theravada.

C. Nirvana.

D. Maharaja.

_______ **19.** Ancient mariners called Southeast Asia

A. the pepper islands.

B. the golden islands.

C. Angkor.

D. Indonesia.

_______ **20.** Pagan, the first great Burmese state, adopted

A. Chinese culture.

B. Islam.

C. Indian institutions.

D. Chinese political ideas.

DIRECTIONS: Short Answer Answer each of the following questions on a separate piece of paper.

> "At the end of three days you reach the noble and magnificent city of Kin-sai, a name that signifies 'the celestial city,' and which it merits from its preeminence to all others in the world, in point of grandeur and beauty, as well as from its abundant delights, which might lead an inhabitant to imagine himself in paradise."
>
> —Marco Polo, late thirteenth century

21. Marco Polo was writing about the Song capital of Hangzhou. Using details from the chapter, explain what developments in Chinese society would have influenced Marco Polo's impression of Hangzhou. How did Marco Polo's impression of China compare with the lives of most Chinese citizens?

> "The people are like birds and beasts; they wear their hair tied up and go barefoot, while for clothing they simply cut a hole in a piece of cloth for their head or they fasten their garments on the left side. It is useless to try to change them."
>
> —Chinese official, *The Birth of Vietnam*

22. This quotation is one Chinese official's description of Vietnam. Explain the historical significance of this quotation. What factors contributed to tension between China and Vietnam? How did Vietnam eventually develop its own state and culture?

Chapter 11 Test, Form B

networks

Civilizations of East Asia

DIRECTIONS: Short Answer Answer each of the following questions on a separate piece of paper.

> "2.14 The Master [Confucius] said, 'The gentleman is broad and not partial; the petty person is partial and not broad.'
> "2.15 The Master said, 'If you learn without thinking about that you have learned, you will be lost. If you think without learning, however, you will fall into danger.'
> "2.16 The Master said, 'Working from the wrong starting point will lead to nothing but harm.'"
>
> —Confucius, *The Analects*, 551–479 A.D.

1. What does Confucius think good students will do?

State	Time Frame	Cultural Influence(s)	Economic Base
Vietnam	Conquered by China in 111 B.C.; independent in A.D. 939	China, Confucianism	Agriculture
Angkor	Arose in 9th century; destroyed by Thailand in 1432	India	Agriculture
Thailand	Thai people first appeared in 6th century, settling in area of present-day Thailand in 15th century	India, Buddhism	Agriculture
Burma (Pagan)	11th–13th centuries	India, Buddhism	Agriculture, sea trade
Malay			
Srivijaya	8th century	India	Sea trade
Sailendra	8th century	India	Agriculture
Majapahit	13th-15th centuries	Islam	Trade, agriculture
Melaka	15th century	Islam	Sea trade

2. Which Malay state lasted for the longest period of time? Using the chart, name one possible reason why this is the case.

3. How does geography affect different economies? Use information from the chart to support your answer.

The Mongol Empire, 1294

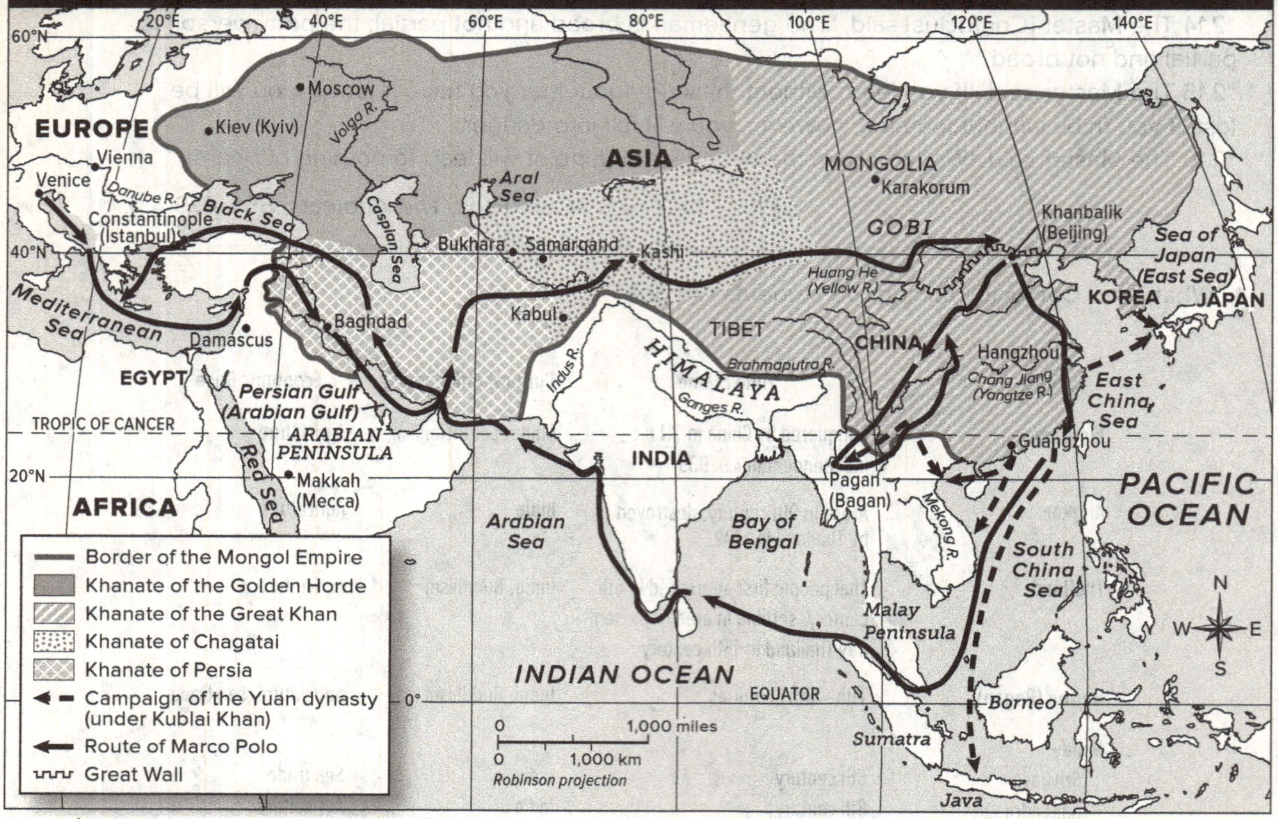

4. Based on the map, what geographic features allowed religious and other cultural ideas to flow into India from the northwest rather than from the northeast or southeast?

5. Based on the map, draw conclusions about the extent of Mongol influence on Asia.

DIRECTIONS: Essay Answer the following question on a separate piece of paper.

6. Between 220 and 1500, empires in East Asia fluctuated, both crumbling and developing as a result of contact with other cultures. Using what you learned about the civilizations of East Asia, explain the chapter's Enduring Understanding statement: *Contact between cultures can influence government, religion, and trade.*

NAME_______________________________ DATE _______________ CLASS _____________

Lesson Quiz 12-1

networks

Crusades and Culture in the Middle Ages

DIRECTIONS: Matching Match each item with the correct statement below.

_______ **1.** territories in central Italy controlled by the pope

_______ **2.** appointment of church officials by secular rulers

_______ **3.** Christian rites

_______ **4.** Holy Office to deal with heretics

_______ **5.** objects connected with saints

A. sacraments

B. Inquisition

C. Papal States

D. relics

E. lay investiture

DIRECTIONS: Multiple Choice Indicate the answer choice that best completes the statement or answers the question.

_______ **6.** The most difficult shrine for most Christians to make a pilgrimage to was in

A. Rome.

B. Jerusalem.

C. Worms.

D. Santiago de Compostela.

_______ **7.** The Cistercian order was founded by monks who wanted to

A. stay in their monasteries.

B. follow a strict, spiritual life.

C. have an easier life than in the harsh Benedictine order.

D. unite the Franciscan and Dominican orders.

_______ **8.** The order most strongly associated with the court called the Inquisition was

A. the Dominicans.

B. the Benedictines.

C. the Cistercians.

D. the Franciscans.

_______ **9.** Convents provided a freedom and support that was unusual for the time for women who

A. wanted to live alone.

B. were intellectuals.

C. expected to marry.

D. owned shops.

_______ **10.** The interdict was an effective political weapon for Pope Innocent III because

A. it forced people to remain married.

B. it prevented priests from giving anyone the sacrament.

C. it proved how powerful the pope was.

D. people affected by the interdict would put pressure on their rulers to agree to the Church's demands.

NAME______________________ DATE ______________ CLASS __________

Lesson Quiz 12-2

networks

Crusades and Culture in the Middle Ages

DIRECTIONS: Modified True/False In the blank, indicate whether the statement is true (T) or false (F). If false edit the statement to make it a true statement.

________ **1.** The idea for the Crusades was born when the Byzantine emperor Alexius I Comnenus asked for help fighting the Ottoman Turks.

____

____

________ **2.** Richard the Lionhearted worked out a compromise with Saladin that allowed Christians to visit Jerusalem.

____

____

________ **3.** As leader of one of the last Crusades, King Louis IX of France defeated the sultan of Egypt.

____

____

DIRECTIONS: Multiple Choice Indicate the answer choice that best completes the statement or answers the question.

________ **4.** As the First Crusade began, Pope Urban II promised the people that

A. the sins of anyone killed on the Crusade would instantly be forgiven.

B. those who fought well would be given a title.

C. all crusaders would be well paid.

D. no one who participated in the Crusade would be killed.

________ **5.** The city that both Muslims and Christians most wanted to control was

A. Venice. **C.** Marseilles.

B. Constantinople. **D.** Jerusalem.

________ **6.** The Muslim leader whose rise to power in the late twelfth century sparked the Third Crusade was named

A. Saladin. **C.** Barbarossa.

B. Alexius I Comnenus. **D.** Baybars.

________ **7.** Which of the following was a result of the Crusades?

A. the breakdown of feudalism

B. the rise of the Byzantine Empire

C. the expulsion of the Muslims from the Holy Land

D. improved relations with the Jews

NAME ______________________ DATE ______________ CLASS __________

Lesson Quiz 12-3

networks

Crusades and Culture in the Middle Ages

DIRECTIONS: Completion Enter the appropriate word(s) to complete the statement.

1. The word ______________________ is derived from the Latin word for "corporation."

2. The language of everyday speech is known as the ______________________.

3. The ______________________ architectural style is characterized by soaring ribbed vaults and pointed arches.

4. The author of *Summa Theologica,* ______________________, is known for his efforts to reconcile Aristotle's writings with Christian ideas.

5. In Geoffrey Chaucer's well-known work, ______________________, a group of travelers on a pilgrimage entertain one another with stories.

DIRECTIONS: Multiple Choice Indicate the answer choice that best completes the statement or answers the question.

_________ **6.** An example of the vernacular literature of the Middle Ages is

A. the *Proslogion* by Anselm of Canterbury.
B. Aristotle's *Summa Theologica*.
C. Roger Bacon's *Opus Majus*.
D. *The Canterbury Tales* by Geoffrey Chaucer.

_________ **7.** Heroic epic poems usually described

A. the lives of saints.
B. Aristotle's works.
C. battles and political contests.
D. love for a lady.

_________ **8.** The main goal of scholasticism was to

A. study religion and God.
B. try to reconcile Christian teachings and the works of ancient philosophers.
C. reform all the sciences.
D. determine what is inherently good or evil.

_________ **9.** Thomas Aquinas would disagree that

A. both reason and faith can reveal truths.
B. using pure reason can reveal a truth about the physical world.
C. it is important to cite opposing opinions along with one's own.
D. truths can conflict with one another.

NAME____ DATE __________________ CLASS ____________

Lesson Quiz 12-4

networks

Crusades and Culture in the Middle Ages

DIRECTIONS: Modified True/False In the blank, indicate whether the statement is true (T) or false (F). If false edit the statement to make it a true statement.

_________ **1.** King Louis XI, who did much to increase France's power after the Hundred Years' War, was often called the Spider.

____

_________ **2.** During the Great Schism, as many as four men claimed to be the pope at the same time.

____

_________ **3.** The Hundred Years' War got its name because the war lasted for exactly a century.

____

_________ **4.** Ferdinand and Isabella made Catholicism the only accepted religion in Spain and expelled Jews and Muslims who would not convert.

____

DIRECTIONS: Multiple Choice Indicate the answer choice that best completes the statement or answers the question.

_________ **5.** Which of the following was a consequence of the plague?

A. more rent income for landlords
B. strengthening of the institution of serfdom
C. increase in the number of workers
D. higher wages for laborers

_________ **6.** The king who engineered the election of a Frenchman, Clement V, as pope was

A. Gregory IX.
B. Philip IV.
C. Henry V.
D. Louis XI.

_________ **7.** The conflicts between nobles in England who sought to control the monarchy are known as the

A. Wars of the Magnolias.
B. Hundred Years' War.
C. War of England.
D. Wars of the Roses.

_________ **8.** In the late Middle Ages, which country pursued a policy of religious conformity?

A. England
B. France
C. the Holy Roman Empire
D. Spain

NAME_____________________________________ DATE _________________ CLASS __________

Chapter 12 Test, Form A

networks

Crusades and Culture in the Middle Ages

DIRECTIONS: Matching Match each item with the correct statement below.

_________ **1.** an unjust or untrue statement intended to create a negative impression of someone

_________ **2.** forbids priests from giving the sacraments to a certain group of people

_________ **3.** court created by the Church to find and try heretics

_________ **4.** an annual direct tax, usually on land or property

_________ **5.** composer and important contributor to Gregorian chant

_________ **6.** a historian of the Byzantine Empire

_________ **7.** defeated the French at the Battle of Agincourt

_________ **8.** those who do not share a certain religious view

_________ **9.** Italian city where the first European university was established

_________ **10.** the plagues that struck Europe in the 14th century

A. Inquisition

B. interdict

C. Black Death

D. Hildegard of Bingen

E. taille

F. Henry V

G. infidels

H. libel

I. Bologna

J. Anna Comnena

DIRECTIONS: Multiple Choice Indicate the answer choice that best completes the statement or answers the question.

_________ **11.** To explain his idea of a holy war to the people, Pope Urban II called Christians together at

A. the Council of Clermont.

B. the *Summa Theologica*.

C. the Byzantine Empire.

D. the Concordat of Worms.

_______ **12.** Born to a wealthy merchant family, Francis of Assisi

A. used his social status to improve the lives of women.

B. eventually abandoned all worldly goods and material pursuits to live and preach in poverty.

C. was both a successful, wealthy merchant and a very popular poet.

D. gave up his claim to the family fortunes to join the Benedictine monastic order.

_______ **13.** Dominic de Guzmán believed the best way to attack heresy was

A. to lead a new Crusade against the Muslims in the Holy Land.

B. by purging the cities of all old people who did not strictly follow Church doctrines.

C. to impose interdicts against kingdoms in which heresy was tolerated.

D. to form a new religious order of men who lived lives of poverty and preached effectively.

_______ **14.** The chief aim of ______________ was to harmonize Christian teachings with the works of the Greek philosophers.

A. Francis of Assisi

B. the *chanson de geste*

C. scholasticism

D. theology

_______ **15.** Which of the following was written in the language of everyday speech in a particular region?

A. vernacular literature

B. biblical literature

C. philosophical literature

D. complex literature

_______ **16.** Joan of Arc brought the Hundred Years' War to a decisive turning point by

A. spying on the English armies.

B. inspiring the French with her faith.

C. fleeing to the English.

D. seducing Charles.

_______ **17.** The introduction of large stained-glass windows into the walls of churches was made possible by builders' development of

A. cross-shaped floor plans.

B. ribbed vaults and flying buttresses.

C. barrel vaults and massive pillars.

D. flat wooden roofs.

_______ **18.** The Bubonic plague was spread by

A. an overall drop in temperatures known as a "little ice age."

B. poisoned water from the town wells.

C. the Great Famine.

D. rats infested with fleas carrying the bacterium.

_______ **19.** The popes' behavior during the Great Schism caused people like John Wyclif and John Hus to

A. criticize the popes for their corruption and abuse of power.

B. found new monastic orders.

C. swear their allegiance to the popes who lived in Avignon, France.

D. attempt to reconcile Christian teachings with the ideas of the Greek philosophers.

_______ **20.** Spain's two strongest kingdoms, Castile and Aragon, were united when

A. the Seljuk Turks invaded Spain.

B. the Jews were expelled.

C. Czar Ivan III came to power in Russia.

D. Isabella married Ferdinand.

DIRECTIONS: Short Answer Answer each of the following questions.

21. What changes in the power of the Church led to the establishment of the Inquisition, and what was the Inquisition for?

____

____

____

____

____

"Here reign the successors of the poor fisherman of Galilee; they have strangely forgotten their origin. I am astounded . . . to see these men loaded with gold and clad in purple, boasting of the spoils of princes and nations."

—Petrarch, Italian poet, in a letter to a friend

22. In this letter, Petrarch complains about the popes who have set themselves up in Avignon. What is the name of this particular historical event and who are the major players? Explain why Petrarch is upset and tell how the situation was eventually resolved.

____

____

____

____

____

"Now, on account of our sins, the sacrilegious enemies of the cross have begun to show their faces. . . . What are you doing, you servants of the cross?. . . . Will you cast pearls before swine?"

—Bernard of Clairvaux, 1140s

23. Why did Bernard of Clairvaux write these words? Explain what caused his anger, what happened as a result, and why the fierce tone is what might be expected from Bernard of Clairvaux.

____

____

____

____

____

NAME_________________________________ DATE _______________ CLASS ___________

Chapter 12 Test, Form B

networks

Crusades and Culture in the Middle Ages

DIRECTIONS: Short Answer Answer each of the following questions on a separate piece of paper.

> "Henry, king not by usurpation, but by the holy ordination of God, to Hildebrand [Gregory VII], not pope, but a false monk. . . . You have mistaken our humility for fear, and have dared to make an attack upon the royal and imperial authority which we received from God. You have threatened to take it away, as if we had received it from you, and as if the empire and kingdom were in your disposal and not in the disposal of God. . . . You have attacked me, who, unworthy as I am, have yet been anointed to rule among the anointed of God, and who, according to the teachings of the fathers, can be judged by no one save God alone, and can be deposed for no crime except infidelity."
>
> —Henry IV, from a letter to Pope Gregory VII, 1076

1. In this letter, King Henry IV expresses his anger at Pope Gregory VIII. Why is he so angry? What is the name that historians have given to the dispute between these two men?

2. How does Henry claim he got his authority as king? What point is he making about his right to appoint Church officials?

The Crusades, 1095–1204

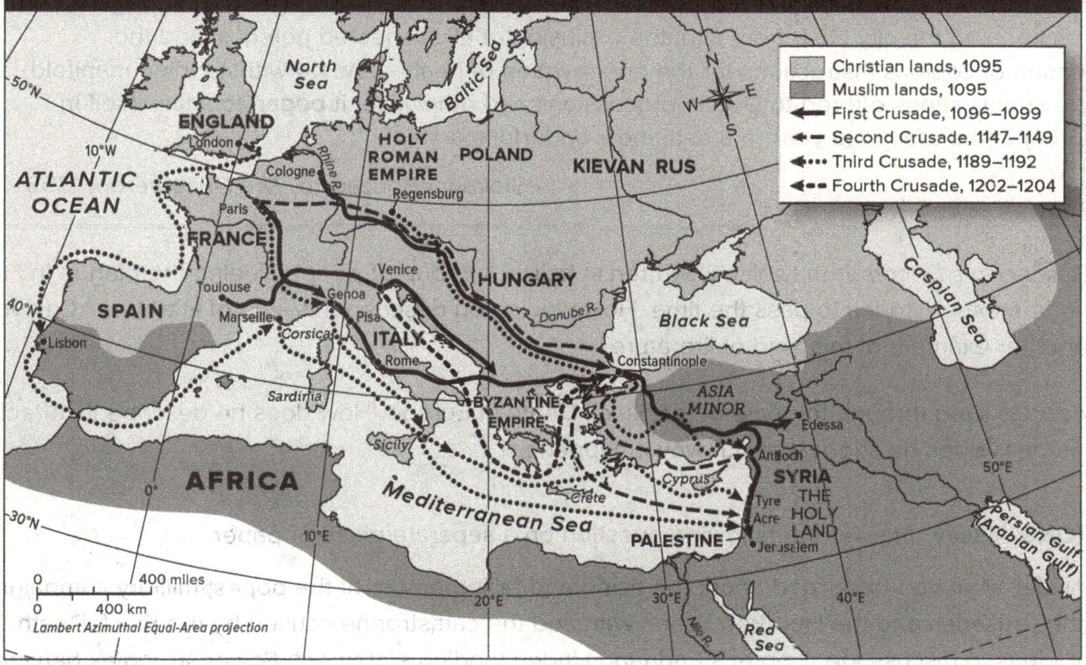

3. Which country participated most actively in the Crusades? How can you tell?

4. What did the Christian armies accomplish during the Fourth Crusade? Did this Crusade help to advance the stated goals of the campaign? How does the information on the map reflect this information?

> "While the victors were rapidly plundering the conquered city, which was theirs by right of conquest, the abbot Martin began to cogitate about his own share of the booty . . . lest he alone should remain empty-handed, while all the others became rich. . . . But, since he thought it not meet to handle any booty of worldly things . . . he began to plan how he might secure some portion of the relics of the saints, of which he knew there was a great quantity in the city."
>
> — about Martin, a French abbot, from Gunther's *Historia Constantinopolitana*, a chronicle of the Fourth Crusade

5. What historical event is Martin taking part in?

6. What does Martin decide he can take?

7. What is the historian's attitude toward Martin's behavior and how can you tell?

> "In the year then of our Lord 1348, there happened at Florence, the finest city in all Italy, a most terrible plague; which, whether owing to the influence of the planets or that it was sent from God as a just punishment for our sins, had broken out some years before in the Levant, and after passing from place to place, and making incredible havoc all the way, had now reached the west. There, spite of all the means that art and human foresight could suggest, such as keeping the city clear from filth, the exclusion of all suspected persons, and the publication of copious instructions for the preservation of health; and notwithstanding manifold humble supplications offered to God in processions and otherwise; it began to show itself in the spring of the aforesaid year, in a sad and wonderful manner."
>
> —Giovanni Boccaccio, *The Decameron*, 1353

8. In Boccaccio's *Decameron,* which is written in Italian, a group of people fleeing the plague in Florence tell one another stories to pass the time. How would you describe this kind of literature? Can you think of another example of this kind of literature?

9. Boccaccio lived through the time of the Black Death in Europe. How does he describe its effects, and what ideas does he suggest about why it happened?

DIRECTIONS: Essay Answer the following question on a separate piece of paper.

10. Consider what you have read about the rising and falling power of the popes; military campaigns such as the Crusades and the Hundred Years' War; and the catastrophe caused by the Black Death. Use your ideas to discuss the chapter's Enduring Understanding statement: *Power struggles between institutions, political and ideological warfare, and epidemics inevitably bring with them drastic changes.*

NAME_______________________________________ DATE _______________ CLASS ___________

Lesson Quiz 13-1

networks

Kingdoms and States of Medieval Africa

DIRECTIONS: Matching Match each item with the correct statement below.

_________ **1.** broad grassland dotted with small trees and shrubs

_________ **2.** East African state with Christian rulers

_________ **3.** largest desert on Earth

_________ **4.** relatively high, flat area of land

_________ **5.** an area in the east with mountains and deep canyons

A. Axum

B. Great Rift Valley

C. Plateau

D. Sahara

E. Savanna

DIRECTIONS: Multiple Choice Indicate the answer choice that best completes the statement or answers the question.

_________ **6.** Western Africa is largely covered by

A. deserts and occasional oases.
B. grasslands and jungles.
C. mountains and plateaus.
D. river delta.

_________ **7.** The area of Africa that juts into the Atlantic Ocean is the

A. hump of Africa.
B. Horn of Africa.
C. Nile Delta.
D. Congo River delta.

_________ **8.** In many African societies, the family lineage is based on the mother, which means that African societies are

A. patrilineal.
B. communal.
C. matrilineal.
D. agnatic.

_________ **9.** In typical African villages, children of less than six years old were raised by

A. adults in either a "house of the women" or a "house of the men."
B. the grandparents of the village in a common children's home.
C. their mothers at home.
D. their fathers in the grandparents' home.

_________ **10.** Islam was first brought to East Africa by

A. Muslim artists from Egypt.
B. Muslim missionaries from Persia.
C. Muslim traders from Arabia.
D. Muslim warriors from Spain.

NAME ______________________ DATE ______________ CLASS ______________

Lesson Quiz 13-2

networks

Kingdoms and States of Medieval Africa

DIRECTIONS: Modified True/False In the blank, indicate whether the statement is true (T) or false (F). If false edit the statement to make it a true statement.

_______ **1.** A typical caravan could have as many as a thousand camels laden with goods.

____

____

_______ **2.** Ghana largely collapsed in the 1100s as a result of being weakened by wars.

____

____

_______ **3.** Mansa Mūsā's actions during his trip to Makkah caused the price of gold to fall.

____

____

DIRECTIONS: Multiple Choice Indicate the answer choice that best completes the statement or answers the question.

_______ **4.** The first great trading state in West Africa was

A. Ghana.
B. Kilwa.
C. Mali.
D. Tanzania.

_______ **5.** Caravans would often take _______________ to reach their destinations.

A. five to eight hours
B. two to three days
C. forty to sixty days
D. one to two years

_______ **6.** What happened as a result of Sunni Ali's conquest of Timbuktu and Djenné?

A. Many Muslims rejected Sunni Ali as an Islamic leader.
B. Songhai took control of the trading empire.
C. Trade routes in northern Africa were closed down.
D. The war debt caused the Songhai economy to collapse.

_______ **7.** The Bantu people of southern and eastern Africa spread techniques for _______________ across Africa.

A. gold mining
B. smelting iron
C. subsistence farming
D. weaving tapestries

_______ **8.** Until the 11th century, most people in southern Africa lived in

A. empires ruled by harsh kings.
B. small family camps that were not part of any villages.
C. stateless societies.
D. villages with no rulers.

Chapter 13 Test, Form A

networks

Kingdoms and States of Medieval Africa

DIRECTIONS: Matching Match each item with the correct statement below.

_______ **1.** group of people in which heredity is traced through the father

_______ **2.** major export of Ghana

_______ **3.** people who worked with supernatural forces to communicate with the gods

_______ **4.** important members of the "fleets of the desert"

_______ **5.** community of related extended families

_______ **6.** highly desirable import for Ghana

_______ **7.** oral historians who preserved traditions and genealogies through stories

_______ **8.** common practice in early east Africa of growing only enough crops for personal use

_______ **9.** group of independent villages organized by clans and led by a local ruler or clan head

_______ **10.** material used to build the Great Mosque of Kilwa

A. camels

B. coral

C. gold

D. diviners

E. griots

F. lineage group

G. patrilineal society

H. salt

I. stateless society

J. subsistence farming

DIRECTIONS: Multiple Choice Indicate the answer choice that best completes the statement or answers the question.

_______ **11.** The "fleets of the desert" were used for trade by

A. Berbers.
B. citizens of Makkah.
C. citizens of Timbuktu.
D. Ghanaians.

_______ **12.** How did Muslim merchants cooperate with Berbers?

A. Berbers carried goods from local traders across the Indian Ocean, and then sold them to Muslim merchants.

B. Berber raiding parties attacked local villages and sold the goods they obtained to Muslim merchants.

C. Berbers created craft goods as they traveled the desert; then, they sold them to Muslim merchants who traded them to local traders.

D. Muslim merchants bought goods from local traders and sold them to Berbers who carried them across the desert.

_______ **13.** Music and storytelling were

A. common only in northern and western Africa.
B. considered holy acts in which only priests and priestesses were allowed to engage.
C. disregarded as unworthy occupations south of the Sahara.
D. used to pass along a community's history.

_______ **14.** Ancestors were a key element in African religion because people believed that

A. ancestors became gods after death.
B. ancestors were closer to the gods.
C. ancestors controlled the weather for their lineage group.
D. ancestors could return to fight as warriors for a lineage group.

_______ **15.** Which of the following was the first of the great trading states to emerge in West Africa?

A. Ghana
B. Axum
C. Mali
D. Songhai

_______ **16.** The kingdom of Mali extended from

A. the coast of the Atlantic Ocean to Timbuktu.
B. the coast of the Indian Ocean to Timbuktu.
C. the coast of the Indian Ocean to Djenné.
D. Djenné to Timbuktu.

_______ **17.** Mansa Mūsā caused Timbuktu to become

A. an armed camp for political prisoners.
B. an intellectual capital of the Muslim world.
C. an oasis for traders who crossed the desert.
D. an outpost for Christian and Jewish refugees.

_______ **18.** Songhai used _______________ as a medium of exchange.

A. cowry shells
B. gold coins
C. large ivory beads
D. small carved ivory statues

_______ **19.** The Songhai Empire was most powerful under the leadership of

A. Battuta.
B. Kossi.
C. Sunni Ali.
D. Muhammad Ture.

________ **20.** Songhai went through a rapid decline as a result of

A. invasion from the south and west by Bantu people.

B. mismanagement by the sons of Muhammad Ture.

C. a civil war and an invasion by the sultan of Morocco.

D. war debt incurred by Muhammad Ture.

DIRECTIONS: Short Answer Answer each of the following questions.

21. Describe Mansa Mūsā's pilgrimage to Makkah and the impact it had on Mali and the countries through which he traveled.

____

____

____

> "Our luck far exceeded expectations. Each of the four pits we dug yielded abundant evidence. . . . Animal bones, rice chaff, and carbonized grains documented a mixed diet. Pottery fragments, spindle whorls, terra-cotta statuary, and crucibles for smelting copper or gold gave insight into local arts and crafts. Walls defined sturdy homes."
>
> —"Finding Jenne-jeno, West Africa's Oldest City" by Susan and Roderick McIntosh. *National Geographic*, Vol. 162, No. 3, September 1982, p. 407.

22. Based on the passage, explain what conclusions you can draw about what life was probably like for the people of Djenné, what they ate, what arts were common, what trades they practiced, and where they lived. Use evidence from the passage to support your answer.

____

____

____

Chapter 13 Test, Form B

networks

Kingdoms and States of Medieval Africa

DIRECTIONS: Short Answer Answer each of the following questions on a separate piece of paper.

> "The land of Zanj [Arab term for East Africa] produces wild leopard skins. The people wear them as clothes, or export them to Muslim countries. They are the largest leopard skins and the most beautiful for making saddles. . . . They also export tortoiseshell for making combs, for which ivory is likewise used. . . . It is from this country that come [elephant] tusks weighing fifty pounds and more. They usually go to Oman, and from there are sent to China and India. This is the chief trade route, and if it were not so, ivory would be common in Muslim lands."
>
> —Abu'l-Hasan Ali al-Musudi, from *Meadows of Gold*, 943

1. Based on this passage, explain why ivory was not common in Muslim lands.

2. According to the passage, for what purpose were leopard skins from East Africa used?

Indian Ocean Trade, 500–1500

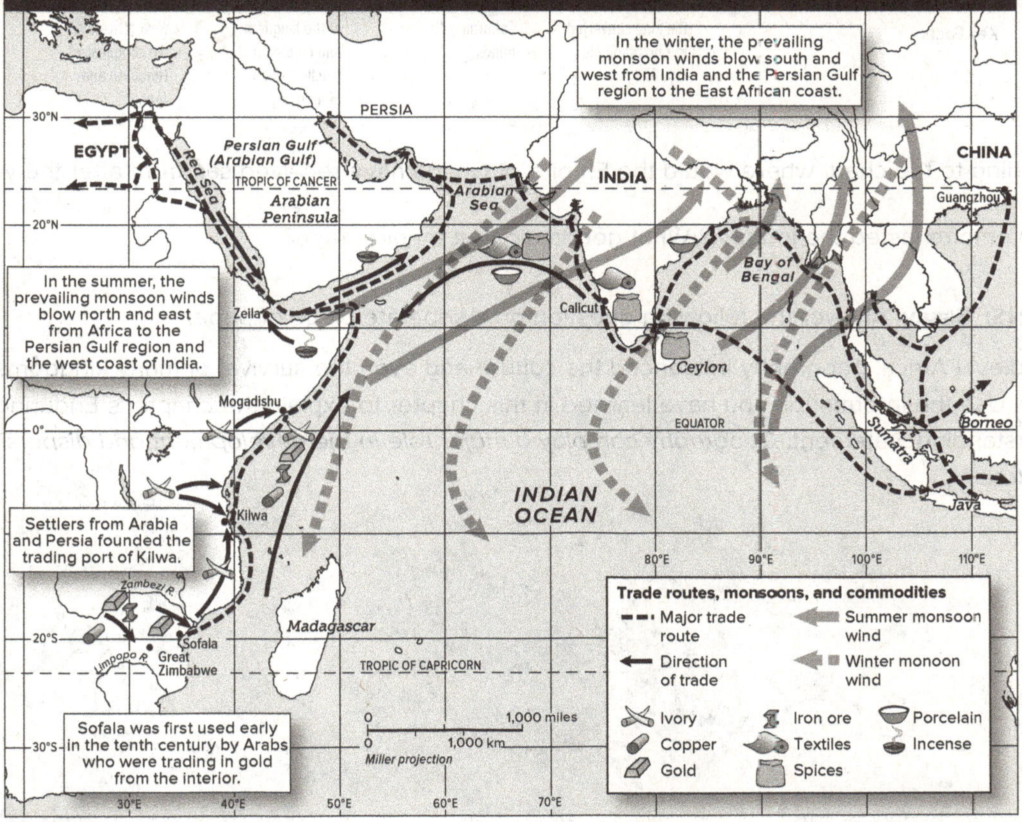

3. According to this map, where would boats traveling over major trade routes from Kilwa arrive first?

4. What is the first major port on the east coast of Africa where a boat carrying goods from Egypt would arrive?

African Trading Empires, 1000 B.C.–A.D.150

	Kush (Nubia)	Axum	Ghana	Mali	Songhai
Empire	Meroë 	Adulis 	Saleh 	Timbuktu 	Gao 
Location	East Africa south of Egypt	East Africa (Ethiopia)	West Africa	West Africa	West Africa
Time Period	1000 B.C.–A.D. 150	A.D. 100–1400	A.D. 400–1200	A.D. 1250–1450	A.D. 1000–1600
Goods Traded	Iron products, ivory, gold, ebony, slaves	Ivory, frankincense, myrrh, slaves	Iron products, animal products, gold	Gold, salt	Gold, salt
Key Facts	Kush lost power to Axum.	Axum was founded by Arab traders; the king converted to Christianity in A.D. 324.	Ghana traded for salt from the Saharan salt mines.	Mansa Mūsā doubled the size of the kingdom and created a Muslim center of learning.	Songhai gained control of trade in West Africa with the conquest of Timbuktu and Jenne.

5. According to the chart, where would the Empire of Ghana have received salt from after the year 1000?

6. Which empire lasted the longest? What goods did that empire trade?

DIRECTIONS: Essay Answer the following question on a separate piece of paper.

7. In medieval Africa, geography influenced the culture and even the survival of many kingdoms and states. Use the information you have learned in this chapter to explain the chapter's Enduring Understanding statement: *Geography can play a major role in the development and dispersion of culture.*

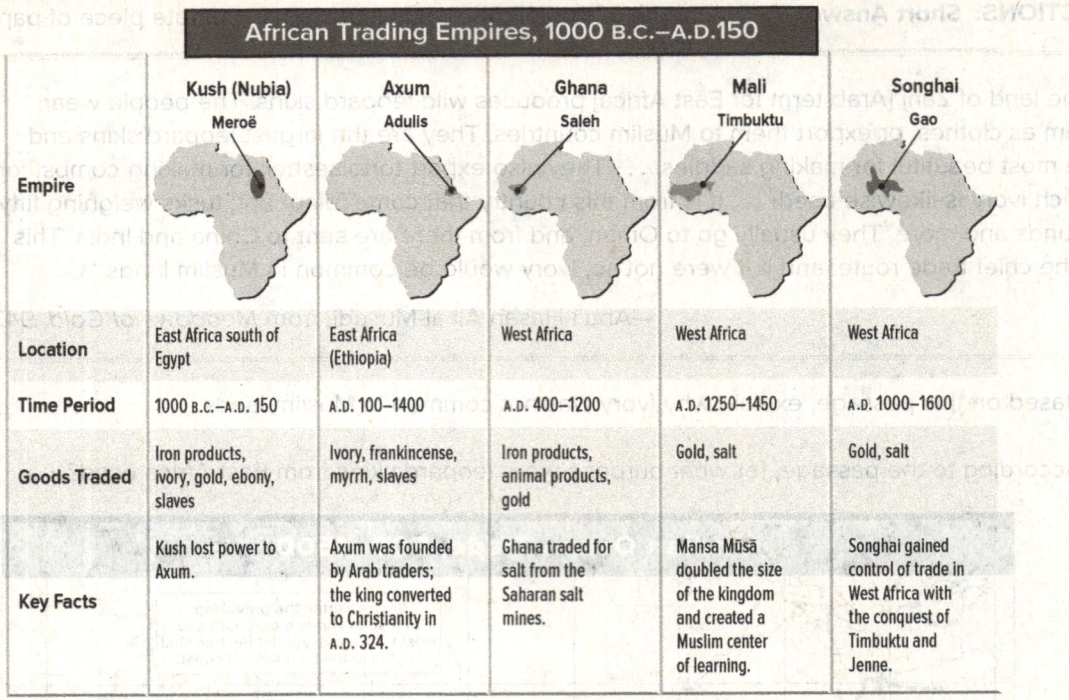

NAME_______________________________________ DATE __________________ CLASS ____________

Lesson Quiz 14-1

networks

Pre-Columbian America

DIRECTIONS: Completion Enter the appropriate word(s) to complete the statement.

1. In approximately A.D. 700, there was a shift to ______________________ in the Mississippi River valley.

2. The most important crops to the Iroquois were ______________________, ______________________, and ______________________, known as the "three sisters."

3. The desert-dwelling Anasazi abandoned Pueblo Bonito, a massive complex that housed over 1,000 people, because of ______________________.

4. The ______________________ of the Maya were built around central pyramids topped with shrines to the gods.

5. Maya nobles ruled over priest-like scribes, peasant farmers, and ______________________.

DIRECTIONS: Multiple Choice Indicate the answer choice that best completes the statement or answers the question.

_________ **6.** One Maya calendar was based on a

A. 150-day year.
B. 30-day year.
C. 365-day year.
D. 1,000-day year.

_________ **7.** Which was the first group to bring metal-working to Mesoamerica?

A. Iroquois
B. Aztec
C. Maya
D. Toltec

_________ **8.** The Aztec Triple Alliance, formed between three city-states,

A. ruled from the Atlantic to the Pacific and as far south as the Guatemalan border.
B. was created after the Aztec fled from the islands and swamps of Lake Texcoco.
C. developed after the reign of Montezuma and the arrival of Spanish forces.
D. was principally democratic and peaceful, avoiding overt military conflicts.

_________ **9.** The king of the Aztec Empire

A. was always drawn from the lower classes of landless laborers or farmers.
B. claimed lineage with the gods and ruled over nobles, slaves, and commoners.
C. mysteriously left his homeland in the Valley of Mexico in the tenth century.
D. frequently opposed the common Mesoamerican practice of human sacrifice.

_________ **10.** Aztec religion was based on a belief in a struggle between which of the following?

A. gods and men
B. the jungle and civilization
C. good and evil
D. men and women

NAME _______________ DATE _______________ CLASS _______________

Lesson Quiz 14-2

networks

Pre-Columbian America

DIRECTIONS: Modified True/False In the blank, indicate whether the statement is true (T) or false (F). If false edit the statement to make it a true statement.

_______ **1.** The Peruvian Nazca culture, which appeared around 200 B.C., preserved some of the Chavin culture.

____

____

_______ **2.** Around A.D. 300, the Moche civilization developed far inland, near the Ecuadorian border.

____

____

_______ **3.** In the 1440s, the Inca brought the entire Pacific coastal region under their control.

____

_______ **4.** Pachacuti conquered his region through trade and a complicated set of alliances.

____

____

DIRECTIONS: Multiple Choice Indicate the answer choice that best completes the statement or answers the question.

_______ **5.** Pachacuti did which of the following to encourage loyalty?

A. All peasants were given land on which they were allowed to farm.
B. Local governors were bribed with gold from conquered cities' temples.
C. Children of regional leaders were taken hostage and sent to the capital.
D. Laborers were moved to the part of the country most in need.

_______ **6.** To create a well-organized empire, Pachacuti

A. divided his lands into four quarters, each ruled by a loyal governor.
B. used new technologies to distribute produce, including maize and beans.
C. created a streamlined democracy that allowed for citizen participation.
D. ended the wasteful practices of forced labor and human sacrifice.

_______ **7.** Which small Inca city was built at an elevation of 8,000 feet?

A. Quechua
B. Moche
C. Chimor
D. Machu Picchu

_______ **8.** The Inca Empire kept historical records with

A. knotted strings.
B. written accounts.
C. calendars.
D. painted bark.

NAME_________________________ DATE _____________ CLASS ___________

Chapter 14 Test, Form A

networks

Pre-Columbian America

DIRECTIONS: Matching Match each item with its definition.

_______ **1.** circular tent made by stretching buffalo skins over wooden poles

_______ **2.** Aztec god of war and of the sun

_______ **3.** system of knotted strings used by the Inca people for keeping records

_______ **4.** a group of related families

_______ **5.** civilization that appeared around A.D. 300 near the Pacific coast

_______ **6.** corn grown by many Native American groups

_______ **7.** Inca ruler who launched a campaign of conquest across the Pacific coast

_______ **8.** Iroquois house built of wooden poles, covered with bark, and housing a dozen families

_______ **9.** city built above the Urubamba River on a high hilltop surrounded by mountain peaks

_______ **10.** site settled by the Aztec, from which they spread their empire across much of Mexico

A. longhouse

B. clan

C. tepee

D. Valley of Mexico

E. Huitzilopochtli

F. maize

G. *quipu*

H. Moche

I. Pachacuti

J. Machu Picchu

DIRECTIONS: Multiple Choice Indicate the answer choice that best completes the statement or answers the question.

_______ **11.** What led to a prosperous culture in the Mississippi River valley in A.D. 700?

A. development of longhouse
B. start of mound building
C. shift to full-time farming
D. end of inter-tribal warfare

_______ **12.** The Maya city-states were

A. regularly at war with each other.
B. governed by townspeople and peasants.
C. sparsely populated religious centers.
D. populated until the twentieth century.

_______ **13.** Which of the following best describes Maya social structure?

A. Scribes and nobles supported absolute rulers who ruled over peasants and townspeople.

B. Peasants, townspeople, and scribes elected new rulers every twelve years.

C. No strict division of labor existed. Men and women shared responsibilities.

D. Townspeople and scribes farmed crops on terraced land surrounding the cities.

_______ **14.** On ceremonial occasions and to appease the gods, the Maya

A. burned large quantities of maize.

B. practiced human sacrifice of war captives.

C. climbed to the central pyramid's shrine.

D. wrote and performed lengthy war songs.

_______ **15.** Introducing metal-working to Mesoamerica, the ____________________ were the first people in the region to work in gold and silver.

A. Nazca

B. Aztec

C. Maya

D. Toltec

_______ **16.** The Aztec government was authoritarian, ruled by a monarch who

A. refused assistance from the nobility.

B. claimed to be descended from the gods.

C. delegated power to merchants and officials.

D. gave tributes to the territorial lords.

_______ **17.** Which people preserved, especially in pottery, the Chavin culture?

A. Nazca

B. Aztec

C. Maya

D. Toltec

_______ **18.** The greatest political power in the Inca Empire was the

A. governor of each imperial quarter.

B. leader of the labor service in Cuzco.

C. nobility from the provinces near Cuzco.

D. emperor, who claimed to be divine.

_______ **19.** Which of the following best describes the Inca agricultural system?

A. pepper and rice farms that were far away from farmers' huts

B. small but highly complex farms that grew vanilla and sugarcane

C. high altitude, terraced farms with precise irrigation systems

D. urban farms managed by women and children of noble birth

_______ **20.** Why did Inca wise men turn historical events into spoken stories?

A. The Inca prized poetry and music.

B. Storytelling was considered sacred.

C. The Inca lacked a system of writing.

D. Written historical records were forbidden.

DIRECTIONS: Short Answer Answer the following question.

> "When we beheld so many cities and towns on the water, and other large settlements built on firm ground, and that broad causeway running so straight and perfectly level to the city of Tenochtitlán, we were astonished because of the great stone towers and temples and buildings that rose up out of the water."
>
> —Bernal Díaz, quoted in *Preserving the World's Greatest Cities*

21. Based on your understanding of the hierarchy of Aztec society, which social group would have been most likely to build these astonishing towers, buildings, and temples? Who would have benefited most from their construction? Use evidence from the passage above to support your answer.

____

____

____

____

DIRECTIONS: Essay Answer the following question on a separate piece of paper.

22. Write an essay that discusses how human sacrifice played a role in Aztec society. Why was this practice important to the Aztec? How might this practice relate to their belief in an unending struggle between the forces of good and evil?

Chapter 14 Test, Form B

networks

Pre-Columbian America

DIRECTIONS: Short Answer Answer each of the following questions on a separate piece of paper.

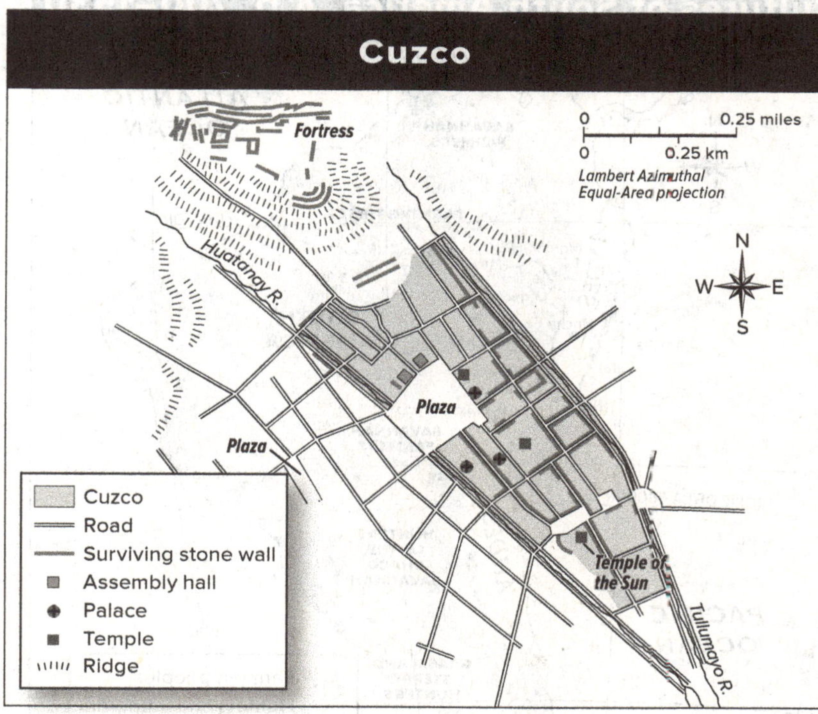

1. According to this map, how many temples stood in the Inca capital at Cuzco? How many palaces?

2. What might these temples and palaces suggest about religious attitudes and social structures in the Inca Empire?

3. How are the religious attitudes and social structures suggested by these buildings similar to the attitudes and structures of other Mesoamerican peoples?

> "Justice was not equal and common to all. . . . [O]ther kinds of punishment were given to the higher-born and rich than those given to the humble and poor. . . . Crimes which, when common people were in question, were punished with death, were, when persons of the noble Inca family were involved, only punished with public reprehension."
>
> —Bernabé Cobo, quoted in *The Last of the Incas*

4. According to Bernabé Cobo, why was justice not equal in the Inca Empire?

5. Based on your understanding of the Inca Empire, explain why these inequalities might have existed.

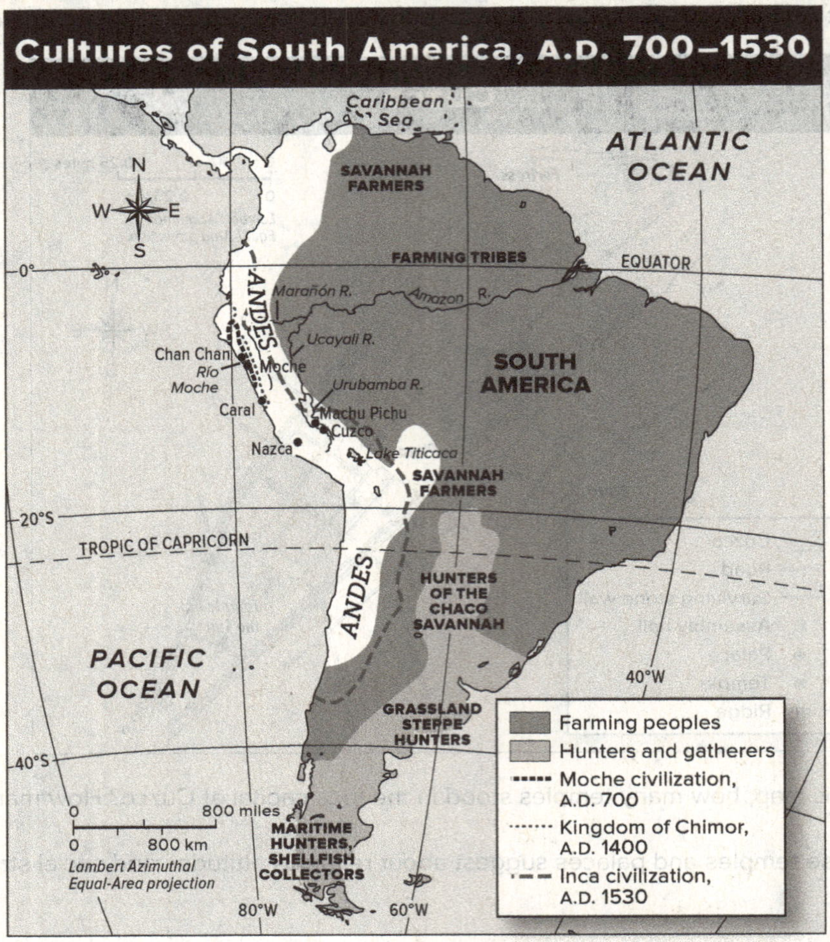

6. Compare and contrast the location and the size of the Moche civilization, the Chimor kingdom, and the Inca Empire.

7. Explain how the Inca were able to create and maintain the civilization depicted above.

DIRECTIONS: Essay Answer the following question on a separate piece of paper.

8. Evaluate your understanding of the peoples of Pre-Columbian America. Consider how their history, environment, political organization, and social structures affected their beliefs, behaviors, and accomplishments. Use these details to analyze the chapter's Enduring Understanding statement: *Early civilizations, even though seemingly isolated, often had sophisticated cultures.*

NAME_______________________________ DATE _______________ CLASS ___________

Lesson Quiz 15-1

networks

The Renaissance in Europe

DIRECTIONS: Matching Match each item with its definition.

_________ **1.** states ruled by hereditary leader

_________ **2.** members of the middle class who lived in a city or town

_________ **3.** soldiers who fight primarily for money

_________ **4.** aristocrats

_________ **5.** a form of government in which the leader is not a king and certain citizens have the right to vote

A. burghers

B. mercenaries

C. monarchies

D. republics

E. nobility

DIRECTIONS: Multiple Choice Indicate the answer choice that best completes the statement or answers the question.

_________ **6.** The Italian states played a crucial role in politics because of

A. their economic power.

B. their allegiance to the Pope.

C. the high demand for Middle Eastern goods.

D. their rule by hereditary monarchs.

_________ **7.** Machiavelli's view influenced political activity because he believed

A. a prince should always honor his word.

B. a ruler should behave based on Christian principles.

C. politics should not be influenced by moral principles.

D. a nobleman should live a life of virtue.

_________ **8.** Which group made up the majority of the European population?

A. nobility

B. urban upper class

C. burghers

D. peasants

_________ **9.** Which of the following is a reason Italy was more urban than the rest of Europe?

A. Italy had five strong states.

B. Other parts of Europe developed centralized monarchical states.

C. The landscape of Italy attracted artists and travelers to the states.

D. The thriving trade networks drew people to the states.

_________ **10.** The growth of large monarchical states in the rest of Europe led to problems for Italy because

A. the Italian people wanted monarchs to rule them.

B. the kings of large states could raise large armies with which to attack states.

C. the rest of Europe was envious of Italy.

D. France and Spain joined together to invade Italy.

NAME________________________ DATE ____________ CLASS ____________

Lesson Quiz 15-2

networks

The Renaissance in Europe

DIRECTIONS: Matching Match each item with its definition.

_______ **1.** intellectual movement based on the study of the classics

_______ **2.** local spoken language

_______ **3.** artistic techniques that give the effect of three-dimensional depth

_______ **4.** history, moral philosophy, rhetoric, grammar and logic, poetry, mathematics, astronomy, and music

_______ **5.** less focused on religion

A. secular

B. liberal studies

C. perspective

D. humanism

E. vernacular

DIRECTIONS: Multiple Choice Indicate the answer choice that best completes the statement or answers the question.

_______ **6.** As a result of Petrarch's finding and using classical Latin manuscripts,

A. other languages became important during the Renaissance.
B. humanist ideas spread throughout scholarly works.
C. people found it more difficult to study.
D. the works of ancient Greeks were ignored.

_______ **7.** Using movable type for printing in Europe led to increased

A. participation in government.
B. wealth for peasants.
C. rates of literacy in Europe.
D. land ownership for nobles.

_______ **8.** The human-focused style of Renaissance artists resulted in art that

A. celebrated religion.
B. imitated the flat art of medieval times.
C. fit in small spaces.
D. used perspective to represent three dimensions.

_______ **9.** The humanists' purpose for educating people was to

A. prepare people for religious lives.
B. produce scholars of ancient literature.
C. make people more artistic.
D. create well-rounded citizens.

NAME____ DATE ___________________ CLASS _____________

Chapter 15 Test, Form A

networks

The Renaissance in Europe

DIRECTIONS: Matching Match each item with the correct statement below.

_________ **1.** state that was the cultural center of Italy

_________ **2.** local spoken language

_________ **3.** intellectual movement based on the study of the literature of ancient Greece and Rome

_________ **4.** state in southern Italy ruled by a hereditary monarch

_________ **5.** German printer who developed movable type

_________ **6.** painting done on fresh wet plaster with water-based paints

_________ **7.** author of an influential treatise on political power

_________ **8.** a member of the middle class

_________ **9.** Flemish painter who perfected the technique of oil painting

_________ **10.** a form of government in which the leader is not a monarch and certain citizens have the right to vote

A. Jan van Eyck

B. humanism

C. republic

D. Florence

E. fresco

F. Niccolò Machiavelli

G. Naples

H. burgher

I. Johannes Gutenberg

J. vernacular

DIRECTIONS: Multiple Choice Indicate the answer choice that best completes the statement or answers the question.

_________ **11.** States were able to function independently because

A. they were located on important trade routes.
B. the Crusades enriched their treasuries.
C. the Italian courts guaranteed their autonomy.
D. Italy did not have a strong central government.

_________ **12.** Leonardo da Vinci was a good example of Renaissance Italy's social ideal because he

A. came from a wealthy family and improved his family's status in society.
B. was a painter, sculptor, architect, inventor, and mathematician.
C. wrote elegant romantic poetry and insightful political treatises.
D. was a politician who initiated important public works projects.

_______ **13.** In The Prince, Machiavelli argues that

A. power has a corrupting influence.

B. people have a basic desire to do good.

C. the ends justify the means.

D. a ruler should act virtuously.

_______ **14.** The main way in which the works of Northern European Renaissance artists differed from those of Italian artists was in

A. realism.

B. scale.

C. craftsmanship.

D. use of color.

_______ **15.** The development of printing using movable type enabled people to

A. become better informed.

B. open schools in rural areas.

C. build libraries and book shops.

D. set up print shops in their homes.

_______ **16.** Petrarch is considered the father of Italian Renaissance humanism because he

A. wrote in the vernacular so that common people could understand his ideas.

B. encouraged scholars to use both medieval and classical Latin in their writings.

C. supported young Renaissance scholars who wanted to study the classics.

D. helped spread classical ideals by reviving forgotten Latin manuscripts.

_______ **17.** The main goal of a humanistic education was to

A. groom students for political careers.

B. promote individuality and creativity.

C. teach people how to lead good lives.

D. produce scholars of ancient literature.

_______ **18.** The war between France and Spain for control of Italy reached a turning point when

A. Spanish mercenaries sacked Rome in 1527.

B. Italian people drove out both armies.

C. the Medici family negotiated a peace.

D. the French army occupied Nice in 1494.

_______ **19.** Venice became an important state because it

A. was ruled by a hereditary monarch.

B. waged a successful war against its neighbors.

C. enjoyed the patronage of the Medici family.

D. served as a commercial link between Asia and Western Europe.

_______ **20.** In Renaissance Italy, most people lived in

A. large urban communities.

B. remote farming villages.

C. small private villas.

D. seaside fishing ports.

DIRECTIONS: Short Answer Answer the following question.

21. Explain how humanism influenced education during the Renaissance.

____

____

____

____

DIRECTIONS: Essay Answer the following question on a separate piece of paper.

> "Everyone realizes how praiseworthy it is for a prince to honour his word and to be straightforward rather than crafty in his dealings; none the less contemporary experience shows that princes who have achieved great things have been those who have given their word lightly, who have known how to trick men with their cunning, and who, in the end, have overcome those abiding by honest principles. . . . A prince, therefore, need not necessarily have all the good qualities I mentioned above, but he should certainly appear to have them . . . [H]e should not deviate from what is good, if that is possible, but he should know how to do evil, if that is necessary."
>
> —Niccolò Machiavelli, from *The Prince*, 1513

22. How does a leader's personal morality fit into the political philosophy espoused in this passage?

Chapter 15 Test, Form B

The Renaissance in Europe

DIRECTIONS: Short Answer Answer each of the following questions.

> "Thou, constrained by no limits in accordance with thine own free will, in whose hand We have set thee at the world's center that thou mayest from thence more easily observe whatever is in the world. We have made thee neither of heaven nor of earth, neither mortal nor immortal, so that with freedom of choice, and with honor, as though the maker and molder of thyself, thou mayest fashion thyself in whatever shape thou shalt prefer."
>
> —Giovanni Pico della Mirandola, from *Oration on the Dignity of Man,* 1486

1. What intellectual movement do the ideas in this passage reflect?

____

____

2. What does free will, as defined in the above passage, allow people to do?

____

____

> "The aim of the perfect Courtier . . . is so to win . . . the favor and mind of the prince whom he serves that he may be able to tell him . . . the truth about everything he needs to know . . . and that when he sees the mind of his prince inclined to a wrong action, he may dare to oppose him . . . so as to dissuade him of every evil intent and bring him to the path of virtue."
>
> —Baldassare Castiglione, from *The Book of the Courtier,* 1528

3. According to the passage, what is the role of a courtier?

____

____

____

4. What important quality does Castiglione say a prince's courtier must have?

____

____

____

Chapter 15 Test, Form B *cont.*

networks

The Renaissance in Europe

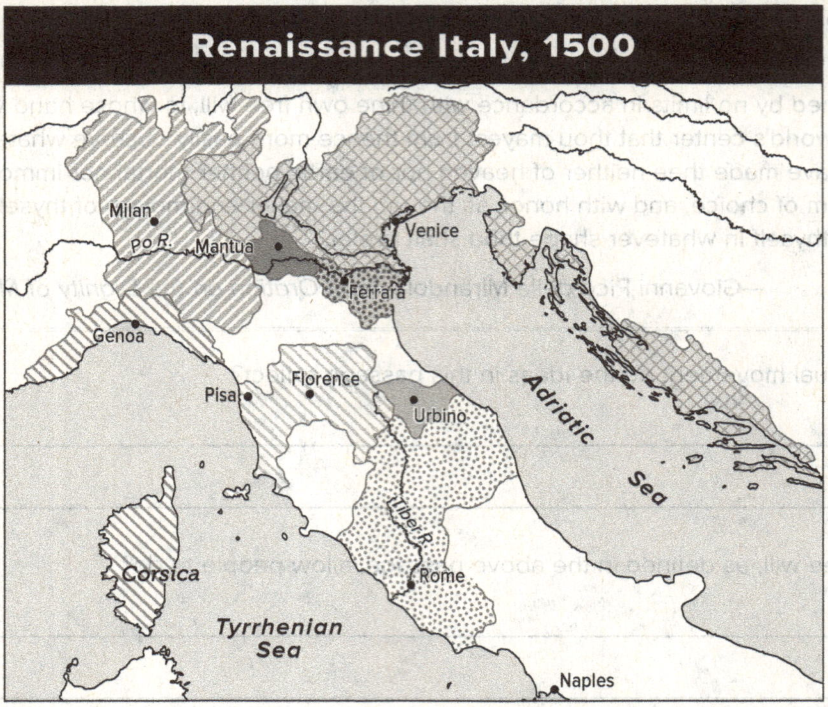

5. Refer to the map above to identify two advantages of Rome's location.

____

____

____

DIRECTIONS: Essay Answer the following question on a separate piece of paper.

6. The Renaissance shaped history by looking back to ancient Greece and Rome and emphasizing individualism. Use the information presented in this chapter to explain the chapter's Enduring Understanding statement: *New ideas can influence politics, economics, and culture—changing the shape of history.*

CHAPTER 1

LESSON QUIZ 1-1

True/False

1. True
2. False—C-14 dating helps reveal the age of an object because living things slowly LOSE radioactive carbon over time. LOSE.
3. True
4. False—Paleolithic peoples probably lived in SMALL GROUPS OF TWENTY OR THIRTY.
5. True

Multiple Choice

6. c **7.** d

LESSON QUIZ 1-2

Completion

1. systematic agriculture
2. domestication
3. cultures
4. river valleys
5. Trade

Multiple Choice

6. c **7.** d **8.** d **9.** d

LESSON QUIZ 1-3

Matching

1. c **2.** e **3.** b **4.** a **5.** d

Multiple Choice

6. d **7.** b **8.** d **9.** a

CHAPTER 1 TEST, FORM A

Matching

1. b **2.** d **3.** h **4.** j **5.** e
6. a **7.** g **8.** i **9.** f **10.** c

Multiple Choice

11. b **12.** d **13.** c **14.** b **15.** b
16. c **17.** a **18.** c **19.** d **20.** c

Short Answer

21. A complete answer should include (1) finding the object by means of excavation at an identified site, (2) examining the object by means of microscopic and biological analyses, such as DNA testing, to piece together information about diet, activities, tools, animals, and so on, and (3) dating the object by radiocarbon dating or by using thermoluminescence.
22. A complete answer should include (1) the city as the aspect of which the speaker is most proud, (2) art, as evidenced in the apparently splendid architecture, as a second aspect of which the speaker is proud, and (3) logical speculation about the city within, such as its grandeur (based on its walls without equal) and its advanced civilization and possibly its government or defense (with sages who know how to lay the proper foundations of a city).

CHAPTER 1 TEST, FORM B

Short Answer

1. Systematic agriculture arose in the Fertile Crescent and river valleys in China and the Americas. Three places to which it spread before 2000 B.C. include southern Europe, coastal northern Africa, and present-day Egypt.
2. Places to which systematic agriculture spread included river valleys, such as the Nile, and places that might have been more easily accessible such as across the Mediterranean Sea rather than across mountains.
3. Early people created these tools to help them with the tasks of daily life necessary for survival, such as getting food and making clothing.
4. The spear, bow and arrow, harpoon, fishhook, bone needles, and scraping tools were all used for hunting or using the animal products. The sharp-edged tools were used for gathering (digging roots); they may possibly have had a use related to using animal products as well.
5. In the map, cities are very close to rivers and other bodies of water. The cities are also very close together.
6. The Fertile Crescent was an ideal place for civilization to begin because there were abundant water sources for raising crops and developing agriculture. People in the Fertile Crescent were able to use irrigation and drainage ditches, which made their crops grow regularly.

Essay

7. A complete answer should include (1) how early humans transitioned from hunter-gatherers to farmers and herders in the Neolithic Revolution, (2) a connection between agriculture and the development of new civilizations, (3) how geography influenced the development of civilization, particularly in the Fertile Crescent, and (4) a brief discussion of new civilizations, such as the Sumerians.

CHAPTER 2

LESSON QUIZ 2-1

Matching

1. b 2. e 3. c 4. a 5. d

Multiple Choice

6. b 7. a 8. d 9. b

LESSON QUIZ 2-2

Matching

1. d 2. b 3. a 4. e 5. c

Multiple Choice

6. b 7. c 8. a 9. b

LESSON QUIZ 2-3

Matching

1. c 2. e 3. d 4. b 5. a

Multiple Choice

6. a 7. d 8. b 9. c

LESSON QUIZ 2-4

Matching

1. d 2. c 3. b 4. a 5. e

Multiple Choice

6. c 7. b 8. d 9. a

LESSON QUIZ 2-5

Matching

1. e 2. c 3. a 4. b 5. d

Multiple Choice

6. a 7. b 8. c 9. c

CHAPTER 2 TEST, FORM A

Matching

1. f 2. g 3. i 4. a 5. c
6. j 7. d 8. b 9. e 10. h

Multiple Choice

11. a 12. d 13. a 14. d 15. c
16. a 17. c 18. b 19. a 20. c
21. c 22. d

Short Answer

23. A complete answer should include (1) Egyptian society must have been highly structured to create a nation-state, (2) Egyptian culture had distinct characteristics, and (3) Egyptian culture was long-lasting.

24. A complete answer should include (1) the Phoenicians invented the alphabet, (2) the Phoenicians taught the alphabet to the Greeks and spread it to the West, and (3) the spread of knowledge from the Mediterranean—and from the Greeks in particular—to the West might have been substantially slowed or perhaps even lost had the Phoenicians not invented the alphabet.

CHAPTER 2 TEST, FORM B

Short Answer

1. The Old Kingdom lasted for 500 years, and 150 years elapsed between the end of the Old Kingdom and the beginning of the Middle Kingdom.

2. Ramses II

3. Sinuhe says that one of the gods has caused him to flee Egypt ("whatever god ordained this flight") by casting him out of his homeland and forcing him to live abroad ("May God grant me peace, may he do thus to perfect the end of him whom he has afflicted, taking pity on him who he cast out to live Abroad!").

4. Egyptians believed in many gods that had power over the lives of humans.

5. A ruler must maintain the infrastructure, treat people fairly and not overtax them, keep order, avoid official corruption, and defend his people against revolts and invaders. If a ruler fails in his responsibilities, then the ruler can be replaced by another.

6. Under the Mandate of Heaven, a ruler who fails to meet his responsibilities can be replaced.

Essay

7. A complete answer should include (1) characteristics and technology used in agriculture, such as the iron plowshare and the use of irrigation, that contributed to a stable food supply, as well as the use of obsidian tools; (2) the political hierarchies within various civilizations; (3) the lasting intellectual contributions of individual societies, such as the 365-day Egyptian calendar, the Phoenician alphabet, and Sanskrit; (4) the artistic and cultural contributions, such as the building of pyramids, palaces, and other massive stone structures, and (5) the role of religion and the family in specific civilizations.

CHAPTER 3

LESSON QUIZ 3-1

True/False

1. False—In establishing his empire, Sargon MADE THE RULERS OF CONQUERED CITY-STATES INTO HIS GOVERNORS.
2. True
3. True
4. False—After the fall of the Akkadian empire, SEVERAL CENTURIES passed before the Babylonian empire arose.
5. False—The Code of Hammurabi reveals that in ancient Babylon a marriage was decided upon by the PARENTS OF THE BRIDE AND GROOM.

Multiple Choice

6. b **7.** a

LESSON QUIZ 3-2

Completion

1. Tutankhamen
2. Amenhotep IV (Akhenaten)
3. Hyksos
4. Kushites
5. Rome

Multiple Choice

6. a **7.** d **8.** b

LESSON QUIZ 3-3

Matching

1. b **2.** a **3.** c **4.** e **5.** d

Multiple Choice

6. b **7.** d **8.** d **9.** a

CHAPTER 3 TEST, FORM A

Matching

1. h **2.** a **3.** e **4.** j **5.** f
6. i **7.** b **8.** g **9.** c **10.** d

Multiple Choice

11. c **12.** b **13.** b **14.** c **15.** a
16. d **17.** a **18.** c **19.** b **20.** d
21. b **22.** c **23.** c

Short Answer

24. A complete answer should include the following: (1) Hammurabi created these laws to help the society he ruled run more smoothly; (2) The legal system represented by the code bears resemblance to laws we still use today (3) However, Hammurabi's laws were strongly based on the principle of retaliation (an eye for an eye, a tooth for a tooth); and (4) Also they reflected the patriarchal and hierarchical nature of his society.

25. A complete answer should include the following: (1) The Assyrians were known for being very well organized as well as skillful in battle. (2) They were good at expanding their empire. (3) However, after a victory, they often treated the defeated people with violence, mutilating captives and destroying towns and food sources. These actions would have made them feared and threatened the ability of their newly acquired subjects to survive. (4) This passage shows Tilglathpileser's pride in having so many horses and chariots to wage war with and in having expanded the empire. (5) It also mentions how he pursued and "laid low" every one of his enemies, taking the violent revenge the Assyrians are famed for.

CHAPTER 3 TEST, FORM B

Short Answer

1. The city-states existed for about 660 years before Sargon established the Akkadian empire.
2. The New Kingdom lasted for 482 years.
3. The empire extends from Libya in the west to India in the east and as far north as Thrace. In Egypt the empire includes lands south of Thebes and it reaches about that far south along the Arabian Sea as well. The empire is about 2,600 miles from east to west.

4. The red line marks the route of the Royal Road. Royal messengers might travel along it to carry messages from the capital in Susa to cities to the north and west.

Essay

5. A complete answer should include the following: (1) a description of the progression of empires from the Akkadian empire through the Babylonian Empire, the Egyptian New Kingdom, the kingdom of Kush, the Assyrian Empire, and the Persian Empire, with mention being made of the important rulers associated with the empires whenever possible (2) a discussion of Sargon's military might and his use of it to create the first empire; (3) a discussion of the Code of Hammurabi and the way in which it imposed certain standards for behavior in Mesopotamian society; (4) a discussion of how the Egyptians learned more about weapon making and warfare from their Hyksos conquerors and used this information to return to independence and power; (5) a discussion of improvements in communication achieved by the Assyrians and Persians through road building and the development of messenger system; and (6) a discussion of how the Kushites used the natural resources of their land, learned iron-smelting techniques, and took advantage of their position along a trade route to build a trading empire.

CHAPTER 4

LESSON QUIZ 4-1

Completion

1. Homer
2. excellence
3. epic poems
4. Phoenician alphabet
5. Mountainous

Multiple Choice

6. b **7.** d **8.** c **9.** a

LESSON QUIZ 4-2

Matching

1. b **2.** a **3.** e **4.** d **5.** c

Multiple Choice

6. d **7.** c **8.** a **9.** c

LESSON QUIZ 4-3

True/False

1. False—According to the legend, the messenger Pheidippides began his twenty-six-mile run in MARATHON.
2. True
3. False—The alliance formed by ATHENS to help defend Greece from the Persians was called the Delian League.
4. True
5. True

Multiple Choice

6. b **7.** a

LESSON QUIZ 4-4

Completion

1. Mount Olympus
2. Plato
3. Parthenon
4. ethics
5. Apollo

Multiple Choice

6. c **7.** c **8.** a **9.** b

LESSON QUIZ 4-5

Matching

1. e **2.** a **3.** b **4.** d **5.** c

Multiple Choice

6. a **7.** a **8.** c **9.** b

CHAPTER 4 TEST, FORM A

Matching

1. f **2.** c **3.** j **4.** h **5.** g
6. a **7.** d **8.** b **9.** e **10.** i

Multiple Choice

11. a **12.** b **13.** a **14.** d **15.** c
16. b **17.** c **18.** d **19.** b **20.** c
21. d **22.** a

Short Answer

23. A complete answer should include discussion of two of the following topics: (1) Alexander did conquer the Persian empire by following the plan of his father, Phillip II, and by bravely leading his men. Combining the Macedonian and Greek armies, he marched into Asia Minor, freed more Greek colonies, and defeated the

Persians at Gaugamela. (2) Alexander did gain personal glory in several ways. He named cities after himself, notably Alexandria in Egypt; he succeeded in behaving in such a way that he has come down in history with the nickname Alexander the Great and there are many brave stories told of him. (3) He did succeed in spreading the Greek language and ideas by conquering such a large empire and paving the way for the Hellenistic era that followed. (4) He did not succeed in fusing the three cultures, because the leaders who succeeded him did not follow his plan of intermarrying with Persians and adopting their culture.

24. A complete answer should include the following: (1) The city-state of Sparta was known for its organization and strict control. (2) Male Spartans were trained from an early age to serve in the military; they joined at age 20 and stayed in the army until they were sixty. (3) A very high value was placed on absolute loyalty to the city-state and bravery in battle. (4) To maintain this discipline and focus, the Spartans rejected all other cultures and had as little contact with them as possible. (5) These qualities were deciding factors both in the causes of the Peloponnesian war and their subsequent victory.

CHAPTER 4 TEST, FORM B

Short Answer

1. The Greeks established colonies as distant as the eastern coast of the Black Sea in Asia Minor.

2. All of the colonies established by the Greeks were along established trade routes.

3. Aristotle is writing about the importance of intelligence in achieving happiness.

4. Aristotle believed in the importance of observation and investigation in seeking the truth. It makes sense that he would place a high value on intelligence and reasoning as a means to happiness, rather than on less intellectual factors such as religious faith or the Epicurean pursuit of pleasure.

5. Many scholars consider Thucydides the greatest historian of the ancient world. By revealing that he has firsthand knowledge of his subject matter because he himself got the plague in Athens, the author confirms his reputation as someone who focuses on getting the facts right.

6. The first Athenians to get sick lived in Piraeus. This makes sense because Piraeus was a port, and the plague would be most likely to arrive on a trading ship that had visited another affected area.

Essay

7. A complete answer should include the following: (1) The mountainous terrain of Greece at first kept communities isolated from one another and gave rise to independent minded, sometimes antagonistic cultures. (2) The country's islands and coastline, however, encouraged people to explore and settle in far-off places. (3) As Greek settlements grew, the city-states of Athens and Sparta became particularly powerful. (4) While Sparta became known for its self-discipline and military prowess, the people of Athens embarked on a route that led to the development of democracy and to a cultural and intellectual flowering unlike any seen in the Western world so far. (5) Greek ideas and literature were spread far and wide by the seafaring culture. When the Macedonians came to conquer the Greeks, they already admired and respected them. Alexander the Great idolized the hero of the Greek epic The Iliad, and hoped to mingle his own culture with that of the Greeks. The Hellenistic kingdoms that came after him also emulated Greek ideals. (6) Even now we still read Greek works of literature, philosophy, and history. Our form of government in the United States is based on ideas that began in ancient Athens. And our language contains many words that have roots in ancient Greek.

CHAPTER 5

LESSON QUIZ 5-1

Matching

1. c **2.** a **3.** e **4.** b **5.** d

Multiple Choice

6. c **7.** a **8.** b **9.** c

LESSON QUIZ 5-2

Matching

1. e **2.** c **3.** a **4.** b **5.** d

Multiple Choice

6. b 7. c 8. a 9. c

LESSON QUIZ 5-3

Matching

1. d 2. c 3. e 4. a 5. b

Multiple Choice

6. c 7. d 8. c 9. a

CHAPTER 5 TEST, FORM A

Matching

1. f 2. j 3. i 4. e 5. c
6. h 7. d 8. a 9. b 10. g

Multiple Choice

11. a 12. b 13. d 14. b 15. d
16. c 17. d 18. a 19. a 20. d

Short Answer

21. A complete answer should include (1) India's abundance of fresh river water and a favorable climate support the agriculture needed to sustain a large population, (2) India's elephants can provide the strength to move heavy objects when constructing buildings, (3) India's natural resources such as gold, silver, iron, and copper provide the materials for industry, and (4) precious stones give Indians valuable materials for trade.

22. A complete answer should include (1) the Buddhist goal of achieving wisdom, (2) evidence of Aoeoka's wisdom in ending selfish goals and suffering by his concern for the welfare of his people, and (3) evidence of Aoeoka's ability to see others as an extension of himself.

CHAPTER 5 TEST, FORM B

Short Answer

1. The Modern Arabic/European number system is the one most widely used today. The number system most widely used today originated with the Hindus.

2. The number systems of the Mayas, Hindus, fifteenth-century Arabic/Europeans, and Modern Arabic/Europeans all included a representation for the number zero.

3. A Buddhist may be able to achieve nirvana in the future.

4. Both Hinduism and Buddhism claim that a person can become one with a universal force.

5. Cloth and clothing, spices, ivory, precious stones, incense, timber, and tortoise shells were traded in or near the Gupta Empire.

6. Changan and Luoyang were located on both the Silk Road and other trade routes.

Essay

7. A complete answer should include (1) the Hindu concept of religious purity and how it justified India's rigid social class structure; (2) the role of meditation and the creation of the Hindu gods; (3) the influence of religion on literature and architecture; and (4) the influence of Buddhist ideas on Indian rulers.

CHAPTER 6

LESSON QUIZ 6-1

Completion

1. Analects
2. human behavior
3. Zhou dynasty
4. Five Constant
5. humanity

Multiple Choice

6. c 7. b 8. a 9. b 10. d

LESSON QUIZ 6-2

True/False

1. False—Qin Shihuangdi initiated the building of the Wall of Ten Thousand , Li to block invaders from the NORTH.
2. True
3. False—After the death of Qin Shihuangdi, THE QIN DYNASTY WAS OVERTHROWN.
4. False—Qin Shihuangdi ruled according to the principles of LEGALISM.
5. True

Multiple Choice

6. b 7. c

LESSON QUIZ 6-3

Matching

1. c 2. a 3. e 4. b 5. d

Multiple Choice

6. c 7. d 8. d 9. c

CHAPTER 6 TEST, FORM A

Matching

1. c **2.** e **3.** h **4.** j **5.** b
6. g **7.** i **8.** a **9.** f **10.** d

Multiple Choice

11. a **12.** b **13.** b **14.** c **15.** a
16. d **17.** b **18.** d **19.** a **20.** d
21. d **22.** a

Short Answer

23. A complete answer should include (1) that although the Han period was one of great prosperity, free peasants began to suffer; (2) Land taxes on the landowning farmers were fairly light, but there were other demands on them, including military service and forced labor of up to one month per year; (3) The Chinese population tripled under the Han dynasty, eventually reducing the average size of the individual farm plot to about one acre per person—barely enough for survival. As time went on, many poor peasants were forced to sell their land and become tenant farmers; and (4) Land once again became owned by the powerful landed aristocrats, who often owned thousands of acres and gathered their own military forces to bully free farmers into becoming tenants.

24. A complete answer should include (1) that the concept of duty meant that people had to subordinate their own interests to the broader needs of the family and the community; (2) Confucius also held that humanity is a sense of compassion and empathy for others. One should not do to others what one does not want done to oneself; (3) The relationship between ruler and the people was one of the Five Constant Relationships by which Confucius believed everyone should be guided; and (4) He believed that rulers should be benevolent and model good behavior and that people should be loyal.

25. A complete answer should include (1) that Qin Shihuangdi ruled according to the principles of Legalism, which said that rulers should be strong, with strict laws, and harsh punishments; (2) However, Qin Shihuangdi took what began as a strict philosophy and made it even more ruthless; the historian Sima Qian noted that he punished men as if he were afraid he would not be able to get to them all; (3) He also did not trust his officials, even though he chose them himself. He employed censorates to check on them and had officials executed if they were guilty of any wrongdoing. From the quote above, we can see that by the end, he considered any criticism, even in the form of good advice, as wrongdoing; and (4) By the end of his reign, he had angered most Chinese people through his censorship of speech, harsh taxes, and forced labor.

CHAPTER 6 TEST, FORM B

Short Answer

1. It reflects the principles of Daoism because it is concerned with how people should allow a situation to "settle into its own perfect place." The best way to be in harmony with universal order is to make action "pure and selfless." The Daoists believed that people should not interfere with nature, so the advice to keep people with still minds, open hearts, and full bellies is in keeping with Daoist philosophy.

2. The only thing that Confucianism has in common with the quote above is the desire to create good order through good behavior. However, a Confucian would say that men of superior ability should be encouraged and trained. Confucians believed that people should work hard to improve their lives here on Earth, and that one of the duties of a ruler was to educate his people and model a strong work ethic.

3. Like the quote above, Legalism was interested in maintaining good order. However, Legalists would not care about filling the bellies of the people or believe that they could be led to good order through example. Legalists believed that people would not serve the interests of the ruler unless they were forced to do so with strict laws and harsh punishments.

4. The Great Wall is between 3600 and 4000 kilometers or 2200 and 2500 miles long.

5. The Han dynasty contributed the most to the Great Wall. Construction began on this wall to keep out nomadic tribes like the Xiongnu. chose officials through a competitive civil service examination.

Essay

6. A complete answer should include (1) that Legalism, Daoism, and Confucianism were focused on earthly matters rather than any kind of abstract divine like other religious systems; (2) The proponents of Legalism sought order and balance by assuming that all people were naturally bad and required strict laws and harsh punishments to keep them in line; (3) Daoism and Confucianism, on the other hand, believed that people were basically good; (4) The philosophies differed in that Daoists believed that the way to maintain harmony with the natural order of the universe was through inaction; (5) Confucians, on the other hand, believed that it was important for all people to work hard to improve the world. They believed that order was maintained through duty and humanity—that is people should place the needs of the family and community above their own individual needs; (6) During the Qin dynasty, the ruler, Qin Shihuangdi, followed the principles of Legalism; (7) The Han dynasty that followed kept some of the elements of the Qin but adapted them in keeping with the principles of Confucianism; and (8) One example of this is the choosing of civil servants by merit rather than by birth. It was a practice begun under the Qin, but the Han added training in Confucian thought and a competitive exam so that they could find men of superior ability to fill government roles.

CHAPTER 7

LESSON QUIZ 7-1

True/False

1. False—Rome's location and its distance from the sea DISCOURAGED attacks by pirates.
2. False—Unlike Greece, Italy's FARMLAND ALLOWED ROME TO SUPPORT A LARGE POPULATION.
3. True
4. False—There was MUCH conflict between the plebeians and the patricians, the two main social and political groups in Rome.
5. False—After the conquest of the Italian peninsula, Rome fought CARTHAGE for control of the Mediterranean.

Multiple Choice

6. a **7.** d **8.** a

LESSON QUIZ 7-2

Matching

1. d **2.** b **3.** e **4.** a **5.** c

Multiple Choice

6. a **7.** b **8.** d **9.** b

LESSON QUIZ 7-3

Completion

1. *Pax Romana*
2. China
3. Virgil
4. paterfamilias
5. Greek

Multiple Choice

6. a **7.** d **8.** b **9.** c **10.** a

CHAPTER 7 TEST, FORM A

Matching

1. f **2.** h **3.** g **4.** i **5.** b
6. j **7.** e **8.** d **9.** c **10.** a

Multiple Choice

11. c **12.** b **13.** a **14.** c **15.** d
16. a **17.** b **18.** d **19.** a **20.** c
21. c

Short Answer

22. A complete answer should include (1) the need to import grain for Rome's urban poor, (2) the desire for luxury goods among the wealthy, (3) the massive economic growth of the period, and (4) the action of good emperors, such as Trajan, who wished to provide a sense of unity throughout the empire.

23. A complete answer should include (1) Juvenal's belief that the empire had eroded the citizenry's participation in public life, (2) Juvenal's contention that most Romans wanted only food and entertainment, (3) an examination of Rome's strict class divisions, and (4) a discussion of poverty and the difficulties of living in Rome, including the dangers and discomforts of urban life and life in the *insulae*.

24. A complete answer should include (1) the bolstering of support for emperors by the Roman Senate's practice of turning them into gods, (2) the Romans' belief that their religious practices were linked to the success of their empire, and (3) a discussion of Roman tolerance of other faiths, which allowed for native groups to retain their religious practices, thus discouraging revolts.

CHAPTER 7 TEST, FORM B

Short Answer

1. The Greeks called this god Hades. The Romans called this god Pluto.
2. The chart suggests that the Romans borrowed many cultural, including religious, ideas from the Greeks.
3. Pliny the Elder suggests that the Romans surpassed all other nations in the quality of their architecture.
4. Other factors that contributed to Rome's ability to excel include their borrowing of architectural techniques from the Greeks, the prosperity engendered by *Pax Romana,* and their development and use of concrete.
5. Virgil suggests that government is the medium of the Romans.
6. Students may identify the success of Romans in the production of great architecture, literature, and the arts.

Essay

7. A complete answer should include (1) the rise of Rome and its earliest cultural and geographic influences, (2) the Punic Wars and their outcomes, (3) the republic, its conflicts, and its decline, (4) the rise of Julius Caesar and Caesar Augustus, (5) *Pax Romana* and Rome's prosperity and artistic and architectural achievements, (6) Rome's interaction and trade with other groups, including their conquest of other nations and tolerance for local customs, (7) an understanding of the importance of the family and religion to Roman social and political life, and (8) a discussion of the quality of everyday life in Rome.

CHAPTER 8

LESSON QUIZ 8-1

Matching

1. d **2.** e **3.** a **4.** c **5.** b

Multiple Choice

6. c **7.** b **8.** d **9.** a

LESSON QUIZ 8-2

Completion

1. Marcus Aurelius
2. tetrarchy
3. inflation
4. Constantinople
5. Visigoths/Vandals

Multiple Choice

6. c **7.** a **8.** d **9.** c

LESSON QUIZ 8-3

Matching

1. c **2.** d **3.** e **4.** a **5.** b

Multiple Choice

6. b **7.** c **8.** b **9.** d

LESSON QUIZ 8-4

Completion

1. excluded from
2. Franks
3. wergild
4. ordeal
5. Carolingian

Multiple Choice

6. c **7.** b **8.** d

LESSON QUIZ 8-5

Modified True/False

1. False—The official language of the Byzantine Empire was GREEK.
2. True
3. True
4. False—Leo III outlawed ICONS as idolatry.

Multiple Choice

5. d **6.** a **7.** d **8.** c

CHAPTER 8 TEST, FORM A

Matching

1. j **2.** c **3.** i **4.** f **5.** h
6. b **7.** a **8.** e **9.** d **10.** g

Multiple Choice

11. c **12.** d **13.** a **14.** b **15.** a
16. d **17.** c **18.** a **19.** c **20.** b

Short Answer

21. A complete answer should include (1) a description of parishes as communities of faithful people (laity) led by priests; (2) a description of bishoprics as groups of parishes led by bishops; (3) a description of archbishops as leaders of groups of bishoprics; and (4) a description of the pope as head of the church. Students may also note that the pope was considered the successor to the apostle Peter and that the bishops of Rome, Antioch, Jerusalem, and Alexandria were especially important.

22. A complete answer should include (1) that both emperors expanded the military and the civil service; (2) that both emperors used control and coercion in setting social and economic policy, with examples such as edicts requiring workers to stay in their vocations and price and wage controls; (3) that Diocletian persecuted Christians, but Constantine converted to Christianity; and (4) that Diocletian divided the empire into four prefectures.

23. A complete answer should include (1) expanding his empire to include Italy, Spain, and North Africa/restoration of the Western Roman Empire in the Mediterranean, based on the information found on the map; (2) Justinian's codification of Roman law in *The Body of Civil Law*; and (3) his rebuilding of Constantinople.

CHAPTER 8 TEST, FORM B

Short Answer

1. He believed that his previous gods no longer listened to him and/or they had no power because they wouldn't help him. He chose to convert to Christianity because when he asked Jesus to help him win a battle, his enemies fled.

2. Clotilda, his wife, has told him that Jesus was the son of the living God.

3. It would appeal to all people, but especially to the poor or powerless, because it defines all people as equal and valuable. It also emphasizes kindness, humility, and love.

4. It would be threatening to Roman officials because it made faith in God more important than faith in any worldly state, including the Roman Empire and its leaders.

5. It stretched as far west as Spain.

6. It stretched as far east as Syria and Palestine.

Essay

7. A complete answer should include (1) a description of the basic principles of Christianity, including the idea of spiritual equality and the focus on humility, charity, and love for others; (2) a description of Christianity's impact on the Roman Empire, beginning with Roman persecution of early Christians and ending with Constantine's conversion and Theodosius the Great's decision to make it the official religion of the empire; (3) a discussion of the opinion of some historians that Christianity contributed to the fall of the Roman Empire; (4) a description of the role Christianity played in the Germanic kingdoms of the West (the Frankish kingdom, Carolingian Empire) and how the monastic movement played a role in spreading Christianity to the Germanic people; and (5) a discussion of the importance of Christianity to the Byzantine Empire.

CHAPTER 9

LESSON QUIZ 9-1

Matching

1. b **2.** e **3.** d **4.** c **5.** a

Multiple Choice

6. c **7.** b **8.** a **9.** c **10.** a

LESSON QUIZ 9-2

Completion

1. father-in-law
2. Madinah
3. Umayyad
4. Berbers
5. Tours

Multiple Choice

6. d **7.** b **8.** b **9.** c

LESSON QUIZ 9-3

Modified True/False

1. False—As a result of trade, the Arab Empire was more urbanized than most of the rest of the world.
2. False—The belief that all Muslims were equal in the eyes of Allah did not lead to a classless society in the Arab world.
3. True
4. False—The mathematical discipline of ALGEBRA was first developed by an Arab mathematician.

Multiple Choice

5. d **6.** a **7.** b

CHAPTER 9 TEST, FORM A

Matching

1. a **2.** g **3.** h **4.** j **5.** i
6. c **7.** e **8.** b **9.** f **10.** d

Multiple Choice

11. a **12.** c **13.** c **14.** b **15.** b
16. c **17.** a **18.** d **19.** a **20.** d

Essay

21. A complete answer should include (1) that Islamic scholars in the Arab Empire made many contributions to mathematics and the sciences that were passed on to the West; (2) that Muslims adopted and passed on the numerical system of India, including the use of zero, and a ninth-century Arab mathematician invented algebra, which is now taught in schools throughout the world; (3) that Muslim scientists also perfected the astrolabe, an astronomical instrument that helped European sailors find their way to the Americas; and (4) that, in the field of medicine, Ibn Sīnā wrote a medical encyclopedia that stressed the contagious nature of certain diseases over 800 years ago.

22. A complete answer should include (1) how the change to Arab rule may not have made much difference in terms of certain people's safety and security; (2) that for some people, though, the change to a government whose laws were tightly connected to a specific religion, the change could be substantial; (3) a description of the social organization of Arab society and what that meant for those outside Islam; (4) the effects Arab and Muslim influences had on women; and (5) how cultures mixed as the Arab Empire expanded.

CHAPTER 9 TEST, FORM B

Short Answer

1. Charity deals with people's relationships with one another. The other four pillars deal primarily with an individual's relationship with Allah.
2. Prayer, Charity, and Pilgrimage all require an individual to perform a physical task, while Belief does not require an individual to do anything physically. Fasting actually requires an individual to avoid performing a specific physical task.
3. The author, Ibn Sīnā, studied the Quran and literature first.
4. The author uses the term "master" instead of "study" because he feels he learned virtually everything there was to know about each subject.
5. Ramadan marks the month when the Quran was revealed to Muhammad.
6. During Ramadan, Muslims fast from dawn to sunset. This period of time relates to the Five Pillars of Islam because Ramadan focuses on simple faith and obeying the will of Allah.

Essay

7. A complete answer will focus on Islam, but may include relevant examples from other religions. The answer should (1) explain how Islam and the *shari'ah* define all aspects of the lives of Muslims, including faith, family life, business practice, and government; (2) describe how supreme leaders of the Islamic faith also served as supreme leaders of governments; (3) provide at least one example of how Islamic beliefs have been used to further political ends (e.g., the belief that soldiers fighting to defend or expand Islam are assured a place in paradise if they die in battle); (4) provide at least one example of how religious differences can cause the collapse of governments (e.g., the split between Shia Muslims and Sunni

Muslims); and (5) explain and provide an example of how incorporating some religious beliefs (e.g., social and spiritual equality of men and women) into a government's law codes can have a potentially positive effect.

CHAPTER 10

LESSON QUIZ 10-1

Matching

1. b **2.** e **3.** a **4.** c **5.** d

Multiple Choice

6. d **7.** c **8.** a **9.** b **10.** b

LESSON QUIZ 10-2

Matching

1. c **2.** a **3.** d **4.** b **5.** e

Multiple Choice

6. c **7.** b **8.** a **9.** c

LESSON QUIZ 10-3

Matching

1. e **2.** a **3.** b **4.** d **5.** c

Multiple Choice

6. a **7.** d **8.** c **9.** c

CHAPTER 10 TEST, FORM A

Matching

1. f **2.** d **3.** b **4.** a **5.** c
6. g **7.** i **8.** j **9.** e **10.** h

Multiple Choice

11. b **12.** a **13.** a **14.** d **15.** c
16. a **17.** a **18.** d **19.** c **20.** b

Short Answer

21. A complete answer should include (1) that Viking raids and decentralized power threatened the safety of the people of northern Europe; (2) a system of feudalism resulted; (3) the system of feudalism included kings, lords, knights, and peasants/serfs; and (4) kings gave a fief, peasants, and military aid to lords, who in turn served the king. Lords/vassals gave food, shelter, and protection to knights, who in turn gave homage and military service. Knights provided food, shelter, and protection to peasants, who in turn farmed the land and paid rents. Students may also mention vassalage, the idea that men provided military service to a lord or king. They may also state that knights were the backbone of European aristocracy and had great prestige.

22. A complete answer should include (1) the invention of the *carruca*, the heavy, wheeled plow, allowed the soil to be turned easily; (2) labor-saving devices, including those powered by water and wind, freed people and animals from doing certain tasks; and (3) a shift to three-field crop rotation left less land fallow and increased crop yield by allowing for both summer and fall harvests.

CHAPTER 10 TEST, FORM B

Short Answer

1. This passage describes the feudal system. The passage refers to a lord and a man who are pledging each other faithfulness and loyalty.

2. Feudalism came into being as a result of Viking raids from the north, which threatened the people of Europe. Also during this time the Carolingian Empire was broken up due to internal disputes, and there was no centralized government to protect the people. Feudalism involved a code of honor that allowed people to make alliances with powerful individuals who were able to hire knights to defend them and their lands.

3. A fief was a grant of land that a lord gave to a vassal. The vassal held political authority over and was responsible for protection of this grant of land.

4. The Western Slavs became Roman Catholic and most of the Eastern Slavs became Christian Orthodox. The Western Slavs' migration brought them close to the Holy Roman Empire and its Roman Catholic influence; the Eastern Slavs' migration brought them close to Byzantine Empire, the seat of Orthodoxy.

5. Kievan Rus was positioned between the Baltic Sea and the Black Sea and was reachable by water. It was also close to the Byzantine Empire.

6. The trade cities are all near water. This suggests that boats were often used to transport goods.

7. The Hanseatic League was a trade association that was founded by merchants in the Baltic/North Sea regions. It provided trade protection and economic opportunities for members.

Essay

8. A complete answer should include (1) the dissipation of the Carolingian Empire and invasion of Vikings causing political destabilization, which led to change in a number of arenas; (2) reorganization of society and politics around a feudal system, which afforded protection from Viking raids; (3) organization of trade guilds and merchant towns, resulting in increased rights and codified laws, such as the Magna Carta, and a new social class, the bourgeoisie; and (4) in seeking to protect the pope, Otto I was crowned Holy Roman emperor, Frederick I and Frederick II tried to establish a strong central state but both ran into problems with popes.

CHAPTER 11

LESSON QUIZ 11-1

Matching

1. a 2. d 3. e 4. c 5. b

Multiple Choice

6. d 7. c 8. a 9. b

LESSON QUIZ 11-2

Modified True/False

1. False—The leader who completed the conquest of the Song dynasty was KUBLAI KHAN.
2. False—The Mongols increased their empire and their trade along the SILK ROAD.
3. False—Cultural advances in China reached their height beginning with the TANG dynasty.

Multiple Choice

4. c 5. b 6. b 7. c

LESSON QUIZ 11-3

Completion

1. central government
2. central rule/central government
3. shogun
4. prose fiction
5. Koguryo

Multiple Choice

6. b 7. d 8. a 9. c 10. a

LESSON QUIZ 11-4

Modified True/False

1. True
2. False—Dai Viet, the new Vietnamese state, adopted STATE CONFUCIANISM.
3. True
4. False—A phase of Islamic expansion in south Asia BEGAN near the end of the tenth century.

Multiple Choice

5. b 6. b 7. d 8. a

CHAPTER 11 TEST, FORM A

Matching

1. f 2. h 3. b 4. i 5. j
6. e 7. d 8. a 9. g 10. c

Multiple Choice

11. c 12. a 13. c 14. a 15. d
16. d 17. b 18. a 19. b 20. c

Short Answer

21. A complete answer should include (1) that the Song dynasty was a time of economic prosperity and cultural achievement; (2) the mention of some Chinese innovations, such as steel and woodblock printing; and (3) a discussion of what did or did not affect Chinese society as a whole, which should include some mention of the class and social status differences that limited certain people's access to the "paradise" that Marco Polo described.

22. A complete answer should include (1) a discussion of the passage's context, which was the years of Chinese rule of Vietnam and the Chinese desire to make Vietnam part of China; (2) the reasons behind the official's view, such as the fact that the Vietnamese people had already established their own culture; and (3) the geographic factors, which included fertile lands that helped create an agricultural economy and geographical barriers that encouraged a separate cultural identity.

CHAPTER 11 TEST, FORM B

Short Answer

1. Good students will go further than just learn what they study; they will also examine or

analyze it. Good students will also be able to evaluate and question what they learn.

2. Majapahit lasted for the longest period of time, specifically from the thirteenth to the fifteenth century. Based on the chart, one possible reason for this would be the diversification of Majapahit's economy, which had a base in both trade and agriculture.

3. Based on the chart, many of the states in Southeast Asia had agriculturally based economies. Fertile river valleys, yet isolating mountains, contributed to the dominance of this type of economy in Vietnam, Angkor, Thailand, and Burma. Also, Burma's proximity to India and the Malay Peninsula's archipelago helps to explain the prominence of sea trade in these areas.

4. The Himalaya created a geographical barrier to the flow of ideas from China to India. Also, it was easier for warriors to cross into India from the northwest.

5. In 1294 the Mongol Empire extended west from Mongolia to Kiev and south from northern Asia to the Himalayas. By controlling this large area, the Mongols could influence nearly all of Asia and parts of the Middle East; however, this large area eventually made it difficult for the Mongols to maintain central control over all their territories.

Essay

6. A complete answer should include (1) the movement of ideas and technology along the Silk Road during China's three dynasties; (2) that Mongol rulers increased trade, especially along the Silk Road, thereby promoting cultural, technological, and economic exchange both to the east and west; (3) that the Chinese form of central government traveled to Japan; (4) that Chinese monks brought Buddhism to Japan; (5) that Chinese ideas of government and Buddhism traveled to Korea with Chinese control; (6) that Islam expanded into India and then into Southeast Asia; and (7) Islam spread throughout Southeast Asia as a result of contact with the Muslim traders who traveled there in search of spices and other goods.

CHAPTER 12

LESSON QUIZ 12-1

Matching

1. c **2.** e **3.** a **4.** b **5.** d

Multiple Choice

6. b **7.** b **8.** a **9.** b **10.** b

LESSON QUIZ 12-2

Modified True/False

1. False—The idea for the Crusades was born when the Byzantine emperor Alexius I Comnenus asked for help fighting the SELJUK Turks.
2. True
3. False—As leader of one of the last Crusades, King Louis IX of France WAS DEFEATED BY the sultan of Egypt.

Multiple Choice

4. a **5.** d **6.** a **7.** a

LESSON QUIZ 12-3

Completion

1. university
2. vernacular
3. Gothic
4. Thomas Aquinas
5. *The Canterbury Tales*

Multiple Choice

6. d **7.** c **8.** b **9.** d

LESSON QUIZ 12-4

Modified True/False

1. True
2. False—During the Great Schism, as many as THREE men claimed to be the pope at the same time.
3. False—The Hundred Years' War got its name because the war lasted for A LITTLE MORE THAN A CENTURY (FROM 1337 TO 1453).
4. True

Multiple Choice

5. d **6.** b **7.** d **8.** d

CHAPTER 12 TEST, FORM A

Matching

1. h **2.** b **3.** a **4.** e **5.** d
6. j **7.** f **8.** g **9.** i **10.** c

Multiple Choice

11. a	12. b	13. d	14. c	15. a
16. b	17. b	18. d	19. a	20. d

Short Answer

21. A complete answer should include (1) mention of the rising influence of the Church following the Investiture Controversy, Pope Innocent III's broadening of papal powers, and the appearance of new, more observant monastic orders; and (2) the explanation that the Inquisition was a powerful court established to re-enforce the Church's power by punishing heresy, often using ruthless means.

22. A complete answer should include (1) the Great Schism occurred when French and Roman Church officials began to fight for control of the papacy and each elected their own pope; (2) Petrarch, like many others (especially other Italians), was upset that the popes led such extravagant, non-spiritual lives; and (3) at the Council of Constance, the competing popes were finally replaced with one pope who was acceptable to everyone.

23. A complete answer should include (1) the idea that the Muslims had begun to strike back against the kingdoms established by the first crusaders; (2) as a result, the Second Crusade was launched; and (3) Bernard of Clairvaux was an outspoken member of the strict Cistercian monastic order, who believed monks should be "soldiers of Christ."

CHAPTER 12 TEST, FORM B

Short Answer

1. He is angry because Gregory has claimed that kings have no right to appoint high-ranking church officials. The dispute is called the Investiture Controversy.

2. Henry says that his power as king comes from God. He means that his right to appoint clergymen was given to him by God and that his powers are not just worldly but spiritual as well.

3. France was the country that participated most. The map shows that most of the campaigns departed from French cities. It also shows that the French took part in three of the four Crusades documented on the map.

4. During the Fourth Crusade, the armies got entangled in a power struggle in the Byzantine Empire and ended by sacking the city of Constantinople. The Venetian crusaders supported the fighting because they wanted to weaken their greatest business competitor. No gains were made in the Christians' "holy war." The map shows that the Crusade departed from Venice and ended in Constantinople, without ever reaching any Muslim-held territories.

5. Martin is one of the crusaders who was present at the sack of Constantinople in 1204.

6. He decides it is acceptable to take relics because they are holy.

7. The author seems to consider Martin just as corrupt and greedy as the other soldiers who pillaged the city. The statement "lest he alone remain empty-handed . . ." describes Martin's thinking in selfish, worldly terms rather than spiritual ones.

8. *The Decameron* is an example of vernacular literature. *The Canterbury Tales* also features stories told by a group of travelers.

9. Boccaccio describes the plague as being "most terrible" and "wreaking havoc" in spite of everything people did to try to counteract it. He theorizes that it was either destiny (caused by the influence of the planets) or a just punishment exacted by God.

Essay

10. A complete answer should include (1) acknowledgment of the ongoing struggles between church and state, with specific examples such as the Investiture Controversy and the Great Schism; (2) discussion of the Crusades as an ideological clash between the Christian and Muslim faiths as well as a political territorial struggle; (3) the devastation caused by the natural disaster of the Black Death; and (4) the subsequent changes resulting from the events and conflicts discussed, especially a discussion of how all the changes of the time contributed to the formation of powerful nation-states.

CHAPTER 13

LESSON QUIZ 13-1

Matching

1. e 2. a 3. d 4. c 5. b

Multiple Choice

6. b 7. a 8. c 9. c 10. c

LESSON QUIZ 13-2

Completion

Modified True/False

1. False—A typical caravan could have as many as a HUNDRED camels laden with goods.
2. True
3. True

Multiple Choice

4. a 5. c 6. b 7. b 8. c

CHAPTER 13 TEST, FORM A

Matching

1. g 2. c 3. d 4. a 5. f
6. h 7. e 8. j 9. i 10. b

Multiple Choice

11. a 12. d 13. d 14. b 15. a
16. a 17. b 18. a 19. d 20. c

Short Answer

21. A complete answer should include (1) that Mansa Mūsā was a devout Muslim; (2) that Mansa Mūsā traveled with thousands of servants and soldiers and hundreds of camels carrying gold; (3) that the value of gold decreased because Mansa Mūsā bought hundreds of items with gold, which put too much gold into circulation; and (4) a brief discussion of how Mansa Mūsā's pilgrimage had a negative effect on individuals who had invested much of their fortune in gold.

22. A complete answer should include (1) an analysis of one or two specific parts of the passage, for example that the "animal bones, rice chaff, and carbonized grains" suggest that the people of Djenné ate a reasonable diet that included meat, rice, and probably some other type of grain; and (2) an explanation about how the evidence described in the passage may reveal important information about the people who lived in Djenné.

CHAPTER 13 TEST, FORM B

Short Answer

1. Although ivory was first shipped to Oman, a Muslim state, it was then transported on to China or India instead of staying in the Muslim territories.

2. Leopard skins were used by people in the Muslim countries to make saddles.

3. Boats traveling from Kilwa would arrive first at either Mogadishu or Sofala.

4. A boat carrying goods from Egypt to the east coast of Africa would arrive first at Mogadishu.

5. Ghana could have received salt from Songhai after the year 1000. It could not have received salt from Mali because the Empire of Ghana had collapsed before the Empire of Mali came into existence.

6. Axum was the longest-lived empire. It traded ivory, frankincense, myrrh, and slaves.

Essay

7. A complete answer should include (1) the four different climate zones in Africa (i.e., midlatitude climates near the northern coast and southern tip, dry climates, and tropical climates); (2) the resources available and geographic features of different areas, and how these resources and features helped define local societies (e.g., gold and iron ore in Ghana helped create a rich trading empire; the arid nature of the deserts gave rise to the nomadic Berbers, and the mild midlatitude climates near the northern coast and southern tip of Africa gave rise to farming economies); (3) how the lack of specific resources in certain areas and the surplus of those resources in other areas caused trade routes to develop (e.g., Ghana traded gold and iron for salt from mines in the Sahara, while east African territories traded ivory, spices, and slaves to traders from Arab lands for products from Asia); and (4) how the development of trade between Muslim societies in southwest Asia and African nations enabled the spread of Islam throughout much of Africa.

CHAPTER 14

LESSON QUIZ 14-1

Completion

1. full-time farming
2. corn; beans; squash
3. prolonged drought
4. cities
5. townspeople

Multiple Choice

6. c 7. d 8. a 9. b 10. c

LESSON QUIZ 14-2

Modified True/False

1. True
2. False—Around A.D. 300, the Moche civilization developed ON THE COAST, near the Ecuadorian border.
3. True
4. False—Pachacuti conquered his region through WAR.

Multiple Choice

5. c 6. a 7. d 8. a

CHAPTER 14 TEST, FORM A

Matching

1. c 2. e 3. g 4. b 5. h
6. f 7. i 8. a 9. j 10. d

Multiple Choice

11. c 12. a 13. a 14. b 15. d
16. b 17. a 18. d 19. c 20. c

Short Answer

21. A complete answer should include (1) the culture's political authoritarianism and its strict hierarchy and social divisions; (2) the probable use of slave or other forced labor in the construction of the buildings; and (3) the likelihood that the nobility were the beneficiaries of this construction.

Essay

22. A complete answer should include (1) the ritual use of human sacrifice to ward off the end of the world; (2) the key role that religion played in Aztec social and political life, as demonstrated by the temple that dominated the center of Tenochtitlán and the ruler's claim that he was descended from the gods; and (3) the seemingly contradictory nature of a moral system that privileges good but practices human sacrifice.

CHAPTER 14 TEST, FORM B

Short Answer

1. There are three temples and three palaces.

2. The presence of so many temples and palaces suggests that the Inca were wealthy and valued their religious practice. Furthermore, the Inca were capable of undertaking large construction projects. Last, these buildings suggest that the Inca were willing to spend great wealth on their nobility and religion.

3. Like the Aztec and the Maya, the Inca lived in a strictly hierarchical society that deeply valued the religious beliefs that stood at the center of its citizens' everyday lives.

4. The nobility were treated with deference. They received lighter punishments than Inca who were not members of the nobility.

5. The Inca political system was highly structured. Inca society was strictly controlled. Furthermore, the Inca lacked a system of writing. Without such a system, it would have been difficult to maintain a consistent and equal justice system.

6. All three civilizations were located on the Pacific coast of South America. All three were in or near the Andes. However, the Moche and the Chimor were significantly smaller than the Inca Empire.

7. The Inca were able to conquer this large region through the leadership of Pachacuti. The Inca were able to maintain their control through their strict social and political organization and their ability to create large-scale agricultural and construction projects. For example, the Inca developed high-altitude farming techniques and built thousands of miles of roads and bridges.

Essay

8. A complete answer should include (1) the agricultural and political developments in North America, including the development of full-time agriculture and the growth of large communities; (2) the growth of highly religious,

socially complex, authoritarian empires in South and Central America, including the Maya, the Aztec, and the Inca; (3) advances in writing, science, and technology by the Maya, the Inca, and the Toltec; and (4) the historical interactions between groups, such as the Nazca and the Chavin or the Inca and the Chimor.

CHAPTER 15

LESSON QUIZ 15-1

Matching

1. c **2.** a **3.** b **4.** e **5.** d

Multiple Choice

6. a **7.** c **8.** d **9.** d **10.** b

LESSON QUIZ 15-2

Matching

1. d **2.** e **3.** c **4.** b **5.** a

Multiple Choice

6. b **7.** c **8.** d **9.** d

CHAPTER 15 TEST, FORM A

Matching

1. d **2.** j **3.** b **4.** g **5.** i
6. e **7.** f **8.** h **9.** a **10.** c

Multiple Choice

11. d **12.** b **13.** c **14.** b **15.** a
16. d **17.** c **18.** a **19.** d **20.** a

Short Answer

21. A complete answer should include (1) the influence of humanist ideals during the Renaissance as education became less focused on religion; (2) the value of a liberal arts education, which concentrated on producing individuals who would lead a virtuous life and who would persuade others to follow that same path; and (3) the revival of Greek and early Roman scholarship in Renaissance education.

Essay

22. A complete answer should include (1) an explanation of Machiavelli's idea that a ruler's attitude toward power must be based on an understanding of human nature, which he believed was basically self-centered; and (2) an explanation of Machiavelli's ideas about the role of the state and how that relates to historical ideas about morality.

CHAPTER 15 TEST, FORM B

Short Answer

1. The passage reflects humanism, the main philosophy of the Renaissance.

2. Free will allows people to mold themselves into whatever they want to be. This freedom of choice means a person has to answer to no one.

3. The role of a courtier is to act as a prince's trusted adviser. A wise courtier will steer the prince "to the path of virtue" if the prince wavers in a decision.

4. Castiglione believes honesty is the courtier's most important quality.

5. Rome had access to the Tiber River, which was a major north-south trade route within Italy. Rome was located on the Tyrrhenian Sea, which gave it maritime trading opportunities with both Europe and North Africa. Because Rome was located in central Italy, it had best access to the other city-states, which increased its strategic importance.

Essay

6. A complete answer should include (1) that the Renaissance was a rebirth of the ancient Greek and Roman appreciation of liberal studies as a road to good citizenship and a way for people to change themselves; (2) that the Renaissance valued both mental and physical abilities, as well as balance, harmony, and order; (3) that the Renaissance emphasized secularism and the individual over the communal, religion-centered society of the Middle Ages; (4) that the art of the Renaissance emphasized the use of perspective and realism; (5) that society became more urban and trade expanded greatly; and (6) that the political structure moved away from one ruler toward the democratic values of the Greeks and early Romans.

TEXT CREDITS

7 1972. The Epic of Gilgamesh: An English Version with an Introduction by N.K. Sanders. London: Penguin Books.; **20** (1)Johnson, Paul. 1998. The Civilization of Ancient Egypt. HarperCollins Publishers, Inc., (2) Moscati, Sabatino. 1968. The World of the Phoenicians. Translated by Alastair Hamilton. Weidenfelt and Nicolson Ltd.; **21** Burstein, Stanley Mayer. 2001. Land of Enchanters: Egyptian Short Stories from the Earliest Times to the Present Day. Edited by Bernard Lewis and Stanley Mayer Burstein. Markus Wiener Publishers.; **30** 1The Writings of Hammurapi (2081 B.B.). Translated by L.W. King. In The Sacred Books and Early Literature of the East. Edited by Charles Francis Horne. New York: Parke, Austin, and Lipscomb, Inc., 1917., 2Grayson, Albert Kirk. 1976. Assyrian Royal Inscriptions, Vol. II: From Tiglath-Pileser I to Ashur-Masir-Apli II. Records of the Ancient Near East. Wiesbaden: Otto Harrassowitz.; **42** Plutarch's Lives of Illustrious Men, Volume I, translated by A. H. Clough. Published by Little, Brown, and Company, 1881.; **43** Aristotle. 1853. The Nicomachean Ethics of Aristotle. Translated by R. W. Browne, M.A. London: Henry G. Bohn.; **44** Thucydides. History of the Peloponnesian War. Translated by Charles Forster Smith. Norwich: Fletcher & Son Ltd., 1919.; **52** (1)Parker, Grant. 2008. The Making of Roman India. New York: Cambridge University Press., (2)de Bary, William Theodore. 1964. Sources of Indian Tradition, Volume 1. New York: Columbia University Press.; **62** Qian, Sima. 1993. Records of the Grand Historian: Han Dynasty Volume 2. Translated by Burton Watson. New York: Columbia University Press.; **63** "Verse 3", from TAO TE CHING: THE DEFINITIVE EDITION by Lao Tzu, translated by Jonathan Star, copyright (c)2001 by Jonathan Star. Used by permission of Jeremy P. Tarcher, an imprint of Penguin Group (USA)Inc.; **72** Excerpt from Satire X. From The Sixteen Satires by Juvenal. Translated by Peter Green. Copyright © 1967, 1974, 1998 by Peter Green. Published by the Penguin Group.; **73** Bohn, trans. "Public and Private Life under the Empire: The Great Buildings in Rome." In Readings in Ancient History: Rome and the West, by William Stearns Davis, 232. Boston, MA: Allyn and Bacon, 1913.; **74** Virgil. 1986. The Aeneid of Virgil, translated by C. Day Lewis. Hogarth Press.; **85** History of the Franks by Gregory of Tours, translated by H. E. W., from Putnam's Dark and Middle Ages Reader: Selections from the 5th to 15th Centuries, edited by Harry E. Wedeck. Copyright © 1964 by Harry E. Wedeck, published by G. P. Putnam's Sons., Colossians 3:10-14. From The Holy Bible: New International Version, containing the Old Testament and the New Testament. Copyright © 1973, 1978, 1984, 2011 by Biblica, Inc. Published by Zondervan Publishing.; **93** A History of the Arab Peoples by Albert Habib Hourani. Copyright © by Albert Hourani. Published by Faber and Faber Limited.; **95** Arberry, A. J. 1967. Aspects of Islamic Civilization. University of Michigan Press.; **96** The Seed and the Soil: Gender and Cosmology in Turkish Village Society by Carol Lowery Delaney. Copyright © 1991 by The Regents of the University of California. Published by University of California Press.; **103** Keynes, Simon, and Michael Lapidge, trans. 1983. Alfred the Great: Asser's Life of King Alfred and Other Contemporary Sources. Penguin Books.; **105** Thatcher, Oliver J., and Edgar H. McNeal. 1907. A Source Book for Mediaeval History: Selected Documents Illustrating the History of Europe in the Middle Age. Charles Scribner's Sons.; **113** Yule, Sir Henry., trans. 1871. The Book of Ser Marco Polo, The Venetian, Concerning the Kingdoms and Marvels of the East, Volume 1. London: John Murray., Taylor, Keith Weller. 1983. The Birth of Vietnam. University of California Press.; **115** Confucius Analects: With Selections from Traditional Commentaries by Confucius, translated by Edward Gilman Slingerland. Copyright © 2003 by Hackett Publishing Company, Inc.The Analects of Confucius, translated by Burton Watson. Copyright © 2007 by Columbia University Press.; **124** Robinson, James Harvey. 1904. Readings in European History, Volume 1. Boston: Ginn & Company., James, Bruno, Scott. 1953. The Letters of St. Bernard of Clairvaux. London: Burns Oates.; **125** Thatcher, Oliver J., and Edgar H. McNeal. 1905. A Source Book for Mediaeval History: Selected Documents Illustrating the History of Europe in the Middle Age. Charles Scribner's Sons.; **126** 1907. The Fourth Crusade from Translations and Reprints from the Original Sources of European History, Vol. III. Philadelphioa: The University of Pennsylvania., Stories of Boccaccio (The Decameron) by Giovanni Boccaccio. Translated by Leopold Flameng. Philadelphia: G. Barrie, 1881.; **131** "Finding Jenne-jeno, West Africa's Oldest City" by Susan and Roderick McIntosh. National Geographic, Vol. 162, No. 3, September 1982, p. 407.; **133** al- Mas'udi, Abu'l-Hasan Ali. "Meadows of Gold." From The Human Record: Sources of Global History Volume I: To 1700. by Alfred J. Andrea and James H. Overfield. Houghton Miffiln Company, 1998.; **139** Preserving the World's Great Cities: The Destruction and Renewal of the Historic Metropolis by Anthony M. Tung. Copyright © 2001 by Anthony M. Tung. Published by Clarkson Potter Publishers, a division of Random House, Inc.; **141** Hyams, Edward, and George Ordish. 1963. The Last of the Incas: The Rise and Fall of an American Empire. Simon and Schuster.; **147** Machiavelli, Niccolò. 1999. The Prince. Translated by George Bull. Penguin Books.; **149** (1)Oration on the Dignity of Man by Giovanni Pico della Mirandola, translated by Elizabeth L. Forbes in THE RENAISSANCE PHILOSOPHY OF MAN. Edited by Ernst Cassirer, Paul Oskar Kristeller, and John Herman Randall Jr. Copyright © 1948 by University of Chicago Press., (2)Castiglione, Baldassare. 1959. The Book of the Courtier. Translated by Charles Singleton. Doubleday.; **152** Burstein, Stanley Mayer. 2001. Land of Enchanters: Egyptian Short Stories from the Earliest Times to the Present Day. Edited by Bernard Lewis and Stanley Mayer Burstein. Markus Wiener Publishers.,